The Murder of Judith Roberts

The Murder of Judith Roberts

The Mark of Peter Sutcliffe

Chris Clark and Tanita Matthews

An imprint of
Pen & Sword Books Ltd
Yorkshire - Philadelphia

First published in Great Britain in 2024 by
Pen & Sword True Crime
An imprint of
Pen & Sword Books Ltd
Yorkshire - Philadelphia

Copyright © Chris Clark and Tanita Matthews, 2024

ISBN 978 1 39908 012 5

The right of Chris Clark and Tanita Matthews to be identified as the Authors of this work has been asserted by them in accordance with the Copyright, Designs and Patents Act 1988.

A CIP catalogue record for this book is available from the British Library.

All rights reserved. No part of this book may be reproduced or transmitted in any form or by any means, electronic or mechanical, including photocopying, recording or by any information storage and retrieval system, without permission from the Publisher in writing.

Typeset in INDIA by IMPEC eSolutions
Printed and bound in England by CPI (UK) Ltd.

Pen & Sword Books Limited incorporates the imprints of Archaeology, Atlas, Aviation, Battleground, Digital, Discovery, Family History, Fiction, History, Local, Local History, Maritime, Military, Military Classics, Politics, Select, Transport, True Crime, After the Battle, Air World, Claymore Press, Frontline Publishing, Leo Cooper, Remember When, Seaforth Publishing, The Praetorian Press, Wharncliffe Books, Wharncliffe Local History, Wharncliffe Transport, Wharncliffe True Crime and White Owl.

For a complete list of Pen & Sword titles please contact

PEN & SWORD BOOKS LIMITED
47 Church Street, Barnsley, South Yorkshire, S70 2AS, England
E-mail: enquiries@pen-and-sword.co.uk
Website: www.pen-and-sword.co.uk

or

PEN AND SWORD BOOKS
1950 Lawrence Rd, Havertown, PA 19083, USA
E-mail: uspen-and-sword@casematepublishers.com
Website: www.penandswordbooks.com

Contents

Abbreviations	vi
Authors' Forewords	viii
Preface	xiii
Introduction	xix

Chapter One	Staffordshire, Tamworth and Wigginton	1
Chapter Two	A Murder Most Foul	12
Chapter Three	The Mark of a Serial Killer	23
Chapter Four	Viewed in the Most Serious Light	39
Chapter Five	Connecting the Dots	50
Chapter Six	A Scapegoat	83
Chapter Seven	The Police Interviews	87
Chapter Eight	The Trial	136
Chapter Nine	The Secret Years	152
Chapter Ten	The Appeal	168
Chapter Eleven	Other Murders Involving a Walling Hammer	198
Chapter Twelve	Friday, 13th	209

Appendix I	216
Bibliography	219
Index	223

Abbreviations

BUDC	Bakewell Urban District Council
C11	Criminal Intelligence Department 11 (specialist unit within the Metropolitan Police, which became SO11)
CCTV	Close Circuit Television
CID	Criminal Investigation Department
Cpl	Corporal
CPS	Criminal Prosecution Service
CRO	Criminal Records Office
DC	Detective Constable
DCI	Detective Chief Inspector
DCS	Detective Chief Superintendent
DI	Detective Inspector
DNA	Deoxyribonucleic Acid (a person's unique genetic code)
DS or Det Sgt	Detective Sergeant
DSI	Detective Superintendent
DSPD	Dangerous Severe Personality Disorder
ET	Enquiry Team
FBI	Federal Bureau of Investigation (United States)
FOI	Freedom of Information
GAD	Generalised Anxiety Disorder
HMP	Her/His Majesty's Prison
L/Cpl	Lance Corporal
MO	Motive

NAAFI	Navy, Army, Air Force Institutes
NCTJ	National Council for the Training of Journalists
OBE	Officer of Most Excellent Order of the British Empire
OM	Officer Manager
PC	Police Constable
PDC	Pre-Departure Clearance
PDF	Personal Descriptive Form
PTSD	Post Traumatic Stress Disorder
QC	Queen's Counsel
QPM	Queen's Police Medal
RAF	Royal Air Force
RSM	Regimental Sergeant Major
SIO	Senior Investigating Officer
SO11	Specialist Operations 11 (specialist unit within the Metropolitan Police)
TIE	Tracing, Implication or Elimination

Authors' Forewords

I will never forget the first time I learned of true evil in the world – the murder of 8-year-old Sarah Payne in July 2000. I was only 6 years old, not much younger than Sarah. I remember the picture of her in her school uniform on the news and feeling a sense of sadness that she was missing. I recall being told at school not to 'go off with strangers'. A couple of weeks later her body was found in a field outside Pulborough. I remember her funeral being featured on the news and how sad I felt.

I grew up in a time when Amanda 'Milly' Dowler was abducted as she walked home from school, murdered by Levi Bellfield, a man so evil he literally makes my skin crawl every time I see his picture or hear his name.

I recall seeing the news of the murders of Holly Wells and Jessica Chapman in 2002 and the disappearance of Madeleine McCann in 2009 featured on the six o'clock news.

I would learn more about these crimes as an adult and for the most part knowing a sense of justice had been done for the victims shaped, for me, a deep interest in cold cases, often prompting me to think about how unfair it is that someone can not only kill another innocent human being, especially a child, but get away with it.

In 2013, I became a journalist, passing my NCTJ qualification and going out into the world as an accredited reporter. My first job was working for a local newspaper in Dorset and over the years my passion and expertise turned to crime reporting. I took up one of my most treasured roles in January 2016, working for national true crime publication *Real Crime* (Future Plc), where I eventually became the investigations editor.

During my three years at the publication, I wrote about some of the world's most devastating crimes and interviewed many who were closest to the cases: my first interview was with David Kaczynski, the brother of Ted Kaczynski (otherwise known as 'The Unabomber'), and over the years I've interviewed many who have been close to some of the world's most devastating crimes from Park Dietz, the psychologist who evaluated cannibal Jeffrey Dahmer, Colin Sutton, the Metropolitan detective who helped capture serial killer Levi Bellfield, undercover officers who have infiltrated dark corners of criminality, survivors of terrifying experiences such as Natascha Kampusch, who was held captive for eight years by Wolfgang Přiklopil before finally escaping, and Rhonda Stapley, a woman who claims to have survived Ted Bundy.

It was in 2017 that I reached out to Chris Clark and his co-author Tim Tate, to interview them about Peter Sutcliffe and their book, *Yorkshire Ripper – The Secret Murders: The True Story of Serial Killer Peter Sutcliffe's Reign of Terror* (John Blake Publishing, 2015), as part of a feature I was writing for 'Real Crime' about this horrific serial killer. I, like them, was looking to reveal a truer picture of Sutcliffe's depraved criminal history. Tim, Chris and I have stayed in contact over the years, our paths crossing frequently, and I'm pleased that we've become good friends. I have always admired and respected their work, both together and as individuals and their diligence in fighting for the truth about the likes of Sutcliffe, who is without a doubt responsible for many more than the thirteen murders and seven attempted murders that he was convicted of. Over the years, my own writing and research has caused me to stumble upon unsolved cases, which have finally been linked to a named serial killer due to a missing piece of the puzzle, and thanks to the diligent work of the police and the determination of the true crime community who refused to let the victims' cases slip from the focus of the public. I can only hope more unsolved cases become solved as technology advances and the determination of the public remains an unwavering strength to the cases that need them.

Writing has always been a passion of mine, but it wasn't until late 2019 that Chris approached me with the research and a draft of this book asking me to help him pull it together. His initial draft told the story of a young girl by the name of Judith Roberts and the devastating circumstances that had occurred one evening in June 1972. I have since spent many hours poring over newspaper archives, police reports, interviewing those who wish to have an open discussion about her murder in the hope that this book could one day offer closure for her family and loved ones. We still hope that some semblance of closure may finally come to the Roberts family. They deserve that at least.

The following year Chris introduced me to a London-based independent production company called Impossible Factual who were in the process of making a two-part documentary for ITV, which was centered around the premise of his and Tim's book, *Yorkshire Ripper – The Secret Murders: The True Story of Serial Killer Peter Sutcliffe's Reign of Terror*. I am thankful that the team, aware of the research I was doing on Judith's case, asked me to partake in the making of the documentary and be their senior researcher. Having spent months working on that programme I came to learn even more and more about Sutcliffe, the crimes he committed, and all the cases Chris and Tim have linked to him. I have seen the very real pain of men and women who have lost loved ones and had their lives devastated because of Sutcliffe.

One thing I would like to make very clear about this book is that Judith's case remains unsolved – the man who was convicted of her murder has since had his conviction quashed and I understand from my research that many people believe that the wrong man was convicted. This is not just a story of the tragic murder of a child but also the effect it had on a man who spent decades of his life in prison for a crime he didn't commit, years he will never get back.

This book puts forward a theory that Sutcliffe was responsible for Judith's murder – a theory that, although we have focused on for good reason, some won't agree with. It was our intention to put forward the theory to the CPS and ask them to look at the likelihood that Sutcliffe was the culprit. His death on 13 November 2020 means that such an option is unfortunately no longer possible. It has been more than fifty years since Judith was killed. I hope that, if we achieve anything from the years spent on this book, it's that we bring some semblance of justice to Judith.

To those who argue Sutcliffe is not the culprit, let me ask you this: who is? Regardless of those who agree or disagree, someone killed another person's child and got away with it. That is something that is never going to change unless we keep reviewing the information.

Secondly, out of respect for the men and women who have lost loved ones due to Sutcliffe, I would like to make note we have eliminated the use of the moniker 'The Yorkshire Ripper' in this book except for where totally necessary, such as direct quotes, of which we have *carefully* selected. Sutcliffe's only significance is that he offers, we feel, a plausible theory to what happened to Judith and potentially many others. He does not deserve notoriety. His crimes were abominable, and we need not synonymies his victims with the gruesome death he bestowed onto them. I understand that for them and their families, every new item – book, article, documentary – on Sutcliffe's crimes is a reminder of their loss. Judith's case shares a great deal of similarities with the thirteen women confirmed to have been killed by him and the many others that lived and helped bring him to justice; we have nothing but respect for them and their families. I wish they felt like they had always been treated as such. With this in mind, we will also not be using the outdated word 'prostitute', and instead would prefer to refer to the women who worked in the business of selling sex, with respect, as 'sex workers'. Some who work in the industry do still prefer to refer to their business as 'prostitution', but to evaluate a case in the twenty-first century we felt it appropriate to adopt language that reflects the current era. Regardless of what you call the act, the idea that anyone would sell their body to feed and clothe their family, keeping them from ruin (as women often did in the 1970s), especially in the knowledge that a serial killer was roaming their streets, is brave but also a reflection that their options were so limited.

I would like to thank Chris for giving me the opportunity to write with him, his friendship has meant a great deal to me over the years we've known one another. My heartfelt thanks extend to his wife, Jeanne, who has always sung a cheery 'hello' anytime I phoned Chris.

I also want to thank Impossible Factual for having me on board the team for the documentary.

Myself and Chris would like to express our immense gratitude and thanks to our friends Chris Heath, who designed the maps found inside the book, and also to Tom Parish who designed the map on the jacket. We would also like to thank our commissioning editor Amy Jordan and contract manager Lori Jones for keeping us on track and for their support and assistance in helping us to tell Judith's story.

A special and personal thanks goes to the wonderful best friend that is my mum, Elaine, who always encouraged me to write and has always believed in me unwaveringly and religiously. Whenever I've had doubts or been anxious about my writing, she has reassured me that I could do it. Without her support I would be lost. I would also like to say thank you to my dad, Mark. I am eternally grateful for your support too and the offer of a much needed cup of tea whenever you have seen me up late at night with my head in this book.

Finally, a thank you to my friends, loved ones and mentors – you know who you all are. If you've allowed me to share my thoughts or offered advice on writing my first book, your support has not gone unnoticed or unappreciated.

Tanita Matthews,
April 2024

In May 1981, Peter Sutcliffe was convicted of the brutal murders of thirteen women and the attempted murders of seven others between 1975 and 1980. Sutcliffe claimed to have heard the voice of 'God' ordering him to kill his victims – many of whom were sex workers. Four psychiatrists diagnosed Sutcliffe as a paranoid schizophrenic. Guilty of more than a dozen murders, he spent more than three decades in high security Broadmoor psychiatric hospital in Berkshire. Before his death in November 2020, he was held at HMP Frankland in Durham, serving twenty concurrent life sentences. His punishment will never serve as penance for the families whose dinner tables are missing a mother, a daughter, a sister or an aunt thanks to Sutcliffe's deplorable deeds.

Since his incarceration, three official internal enquiries have been held: The Byford Report (1981) carried out by the Home Office, The Sampson Report (1981) undertaken by West Yorkshire Police, and the Keith Hellawell Investigation (1981–1992) ordered by Colin Sampson and continued by Hellawell while he was chief constable of West Yorkshire Police. However, key portions of their reports have been kept secret to date. The true motive for Sutcliffe's murders – necrophilia – has been suppressed.

Now, a more recent three-year investigation by a retired police intelligence officer has uncovered evidence that police have long tried to suppress. Its findings suggest that Sutcliffe killed at least twenty-three others as well as another thirteen women who were attacked and survived. All of these murders – dating back almost fifty years – remain unsolved. In three high-profile cases, other innocent men were wrongly imprisoned for what we believe are Sutcliffe's crimes. Their convictions have now been quashed.

For three years, Chris Clark (the author), a highly experienced retired detective and police intelligence officer, has been investigating allegations that Sutcliffe murdered as many as forty-two men and women in addition to the killings for which he was convicted.

The suggestion that Sutcliffe had killed many more people was first made in The Byford Report in 1981 – an official enquiry, which was ordered by the Home Office to investigate blunders by West Yorkshire Police in the investigation into the then unknown assailant. Sir Lawrence Byford warned:

> We feel it highly improbable the crimes in respect of which Sutcliffe has been charged and convicted are the only ones attributable to him.

Despite this sweeping declaration, The Byford Report was kept secret for twenty-five years. It was not released until 2006 – despite the grave warning by Byford, few people saw the significance of the warning.

Meanwhile, an internal investigation by West Yorkshire Police's Chief Constable Keith Hellawell, carried out synonymously with the Home Office's enquiry, identified forty-two separate unsolved murders from all over Britain. Hellawell believed Sutcliffe had carried out at least twenty-two of them. But, like The Byford Report, much of Hellawell's detailed enquiry was suppressed: its key evidence remains secret to this day.

Chris spent twenty-eight years with Norfolk Constabulary. He worked his way up from a beat Bobby to royal protection officer, and CID local intelligence. He was involved in major incident rooms and revolutionised the force's intelligence systems. Chris began investigating Sutcliffe's possible unknown murders in 2012. Using his detective's skills, patient intelligence gathering and with the assistance of former pathologists, the detectives on the investigating team and the families of victims, he was able to identify twenty-three unsolved killings, all of which bore the hallmark of Sutcliffe. In each case he was able to place Sutcliffe very close to the murder scene at the time of their occurrence.

> Chris's patient reinvestigations into these long cold cases have delighted many of the relatives of the murdered men and women. 'I am in touch with many of them,' said Chris.
>
> They had almost given up hope of finding out who killed their loved ones and were living with the terrible pain of not knowing.

Chris's investigation discovered that the police had allegedly discounted – and then covered up – clear evidence of a sexual motive for Sutcliffe's crimes. The convicted murderer always denied any sexual motive, but deep in West Yorkshire Police records, Chris found witness statements and physical evidence that unveil Sutcliffe as a necrophiliac who could only find sexual satisfaction with a dead body – a claim that Sutcliffe himself had always denied, insisting that his motive for the killings came from a higher power – the voice of 'God' who saw Sutcliffe as his weapon in wiping out the sins of sex workers.

Regardless of this, some of the women who survived clearly stated that Sutcliffe, believing he had killed them, masturbated over and on to them while they lay still and lifeless. There was also evidence of semen on the bodies of some of Sutcliffe's deceased victims, and most importantly of all, the investigating detectives on this case had seized from him specially modified underwear which enabled him to expose his genitals quickly in order to masturbate immediately after an attack. Chris said:

> This information and evidence was never tendered in evidence or the apparel produced as an exhibit at his trial – and had never been publicly released until I located it.

Chris continued:

> I have come to believe that West Yorkshire Police were so anxious to get the trial over with that they colluded with Sutcliffe's claims of madness just to get him locked up.

Chris's conclusion was supported by Professor Tony Maden, who was a highly respected former head of the DSPD unit at Broadmoor, which housed Sutcliffe between 1984 and 2016. He believed Sutcliffe was bad, not mad and should have been in a regular prison as opposed to the specialist hospital where he had spent time.

In October 2013, Maden claimed that Broadmoor was keeping 'celebrity' patients longer than they should. He said patients such as Sutcliffe should be sent to prison; Sutcliffe would be in a normal prison if he wasn't infamous.

> We are far too ready to keep mentally disordered prisoners in places like Broadmoor indefinitely, particularly if they are famous ... I think it's about celebrity, I can't think of any other reason why a hospital would want to hang on to somebody when essentially the condition is stable.

Maden thought that these patients could be better managed in prison for much less money.

But the most shocking result of Chris's investigation has been the discovery that three innocent men spent many years in prison for murders he believes to have been carried out by Sutcliffe.

In 1973, Staffordshire soldier Andrew James Evans served twenty-five years behind bars for the murder of Tamworth schoolgirl Judith Roberts.

The following year, in 1974, a 17-year-old council worker named Stephen Downing began what would become a twenty-seven-year sentence for the murder of Derbyshire woman Wendy Sewell in what is known as the longest miscarriage of justice in British legal history.

The year 1979 saw 23-year-old council gardener Anthony Steel sentenced to twenty years inside a cell after a young woman named Carol Wilkinson was 'savagely attacked' in Woodhall Road, Bradford as she walked to her place of work.

The reason for these terrible miscarriages of justice was the blunder by the original police forces and later investigating officers in discounting the clear evidence of a perverted sexual motive in Sutcliffe's killing spree: suppressing this evidence saw them miss an opportunity to link the man who would go on to kill thirteen women and attack several others not part of these enquiries and led to innocent men being wrongly convicted for crimes that they were eventually cleared of.

Within this book, utilising released files held by The National Archives, which include the original pathologist report, scene of crime and postmortem images, and key witness statements, Chris outlines the critical failings of one particular case: the 1972 murder of Judith Roberts, which resulted in the wrongful conviction of Andrew Evans.

During 2012, Chris started researching, with the help of both the internet and original newspaper articles, a number of unsolved murders, which had occurred to lone females throughout England during the 1970s, all having the similar method of a frenzied sexual attack, coupled with postmortem injuries. His conclusion was that many, if not all, had been committed by the same person before and during the series of twenty crimes – thirteen murders and seven attempted murders – committed by this one man, which culminated in the arrest of Sutcliffe on 2 January 1981. Chris's problem, however, was that having identified the same methods and motive within the sample, he could not establish the third element: opportunity.

During May 2013, Chris purchased a copy of *Somebody's Husband, Somebody's Son: The Story of the Yorkshire Ripper* by Gordon Burn

(Faber and Faber, 2004). Upon reading Burn's account, which was compiled over a three-year period (1982–1985), and with the assistance of family and friends of Sutcliffe, Chris was able to pinpoint Sutcliffe's physical presence within the time frame of the unsolved crimes that he was investigating. As a result, on 29 June 2015, the book by Chris and Tim titled *Yorkshire Ripper – The Secret Murders: The True Story of Serial Killer Peter Sutcliffe's Reign of Terror*, was published. Within its contents a further twenty-three unsolved murders and thirteen unsolved attacks were examined and identified as probably having been committed by Sutcliffe. One such case being the June 1972 murder of Judith Roberts, which saw Andrew Evans become embroiled in and eventually wrongfully convicted of. He spent twenty-five years behind bars before being released on appeal.

This murder and the subsequent wrongful conviction were what Chris deemed to be a catalyst for the introduction of Sutcliffe as the most likely candidate for this awful unsolved crime.

Chris would like to thank his wife Jeanne for her support and encouragement. Jeanne has been there every step of the way from when he first started researching Judith's murder, back in 2012.

Introduction

Judith Roberts was a 14-year-old grammar school pupil from Wigginton, near Tamworth. She was described as bright and academic. On the evening of 7 June 1972, after Judith was scorned by her father for her fussy eating, she left home to cycle along Comberford Lane. Her body was discovered three days later in a field adjacent to the road, and a subsequent postmortem concluded she had been beaten to death.

Police launched a murder investigation involving hundreds of detectives. However, in spite of what became one of the Midlands' most intensive hunts for a murder suspect, the killer remained at large for a number of months.

In June 1972, Andrew Evans was a 17-year-old soldier stationed at Whittington Barracks near Lichfield, Staffordshire, but having suffered an asthma attack, he was awaiting discharge from the army on medical grounds. On 7 June 1972, the evening that Judith Roberts was killed, he was a day away from handing in his uniform and returning home. A semi-literate, nervous, and socially awkward teenager, he had joined the armed forces in the hope of a career, and after being discharged he was treated for depression.

As part of the police investigation into the murder, soldiers residing at Whittington Barracks on the day of the murder were required to provide an account of their whereabouts on that evening. Evans said that he spent the evening at the barracks, providing the names of three other soldiers who could verify his alibi. However, police subsequently failed to trace one of the soldiers, and discovered the remaining two had left the barracks prior to 7 June 1972. Evans was questioned again in October 1972.

Following the interview, Evans told his grandmother that he planned to visit the police station because he wanted to see a photograph of Judith. Evans made this decision following a dream in which he saw 'a hazy combination of images of women's faces'. His grandmother advised him against such action, but he subsequently visited Longton Police Station in a distressed state, where he made his request.

During a series of interviews with detectives, Evans claimed that he had dragged Judith from her bicycle, then struggled with her in a field.

Detectives initially did not believe his account, dismissing him as a fantasist, but following intensive questioning they became certain he was the killer. After giving a signed statement under caution, Evans was charged with murder. Speaking in 2000 about this, Evans told *The Guardian's* Patrick Weir,

> By confessing, I thought I'd be able to rid myself of all the crap going on in my head.

Evans' trial was held at Birmingham Crown Court in June 1973. By this time, he believed that he was innocent and had retracted his original statement. Apart from the confession, no other evidence was presented; there was no scientific evidence against Evans nor any eyewitnesses to support or refute the Crown's case. However, Evans could not provide an alibi for 7 June 1972, and a psychiatrist testified that Evans was suffering from amnesia. Evans' defence argued that he was suffering from hysterical amnesia and had cast himself in the role of killer after witnessing the murder, failing to help Judith. Despite this, he was convicted of Judith's murder and sentenced to life imprisonment.

Advised that he had no grounds for an appeal, Evans spent the next two decades in prison before his case came to the attention of the British media and was taken up by the human rights group, Justice.

This was following a chance encounter with a member of Greenpeace while Evans was an inmate at HMP The Verne who passed on details of his case to two producers at Carlton Television. The case subsequently featured on Central Television's regional magazine programme, *Crime Stalker*, and later in a documentary, *The Nightmare*.

Evans also wrote to Justice about his case, they agreed to take it up and he was represented by their solicitor. Evans subsequently won the right to appeal against his conviction in 1997.

The appeal hearing was told that in 1972, Evans had been taking prescription medication for depression and the judges were critical of how the police inquiry was conducted.

The Court of Appeal consequently quashed Evans' conviction after deeming it to be unsafe, and he was released from custody with immediate effect.

At the time of his release, Evans had served the longest period in prison in the United Kingdom as the result of a miscarriage of justice.

Following the appeal, Staffordshire Police said that they had no plans to reopen their investigation into the murder of Judith Roberts, claiming that all lines of enquiry had been followed up at the time.

Evans sought compensation from the Home Office for his wrongful conviction and was subsequently awarded £750,000, although together with other payments he received from them, it is estimated that his compensation was approximately £1 million.

Chapter One

Staffordshire, Tamworth and Wigginton

Nestled in the West Midlands of England, Staffordshire's boundary lines salute the counties of Cheshire, Derbyshire and Leicestershire in the east, Warwickshire is to its south-east while Shropshire can be found in its western hemisphere. In Staffordshire's middle regions, its landscape is low and undulating, compared to the north and the south where the county is hilly, with wild moorlands and uplands of the beautiful Peak District in the far north, and Cannock Chase, an area of natural beauty, in the south. Woven into the greenery of Shropshire's landscape remain hints of the county's impressive mining community – vast coalfields and iron ore deposits that date back to the thirteenth century. Flowing through its fertile grounds is the River Trent, Britain's third longest river, considered an unofficial boundary that caresses the Midlands and the north of England. It is a landmark that symbolises a potential link between the murder of a 14-year-old schoolgirl to the murders and attacks of scores of other women at the hands of a Bingley lorry driver.

Sitting abreast of the county is a glimmering jewel in its crown: Flash, the highest village in Britain. Situated in the Staffordshire Moorlands, it stands at 1,519 feet (463 metres) above sea level. (This record was confirmed in 2007 by the Ordnance Survey after Wanlockhead in Scotland also attempted to claim the record. BBC's *The One Show* investigated the case in a bid to settle the argument and Flash was confirmed the winner, with Cheeks Point being named as the highest point.)

Two major cities dominate Staffordshire's landscape. Its largest, Stoke-on-Trent, is administered separately from the rest of the county as an independent unitary authority. Meanwhile Lichfield, with its impressive city status, is a considerably smaller cathedral city. Major towns that make up its landscape include Stafford (the county town), Burton-upon-Trent, Cannock, Newcastle-under-Lyme, Leek and Tamworth. Smaller towns include Stone, Cheadle, Uttoxeter, Rugeley, Burntwood, Chasetown, Eccleshall and Penkridge as well as the large villages of Wombourne, Kinver, Tutbury, Alrewas, Barton-under-Needwood, Stretton and Abbots Bromley. While Wolverhampton, Walsall, West Bromwich and Smethwick are within the historic county boundaries of Staffordshire, they have been part of West Midlands County since 1974.

Apart from Stoke-on-Trent, Staffordshire is divided into several districts that make up its rich geography: Cannock Chase, East Staffordshire, Lichfield, Newcastle-under-Lyme, South Staffordshire, Stafford, Staffordshire Moorlands, and Tamworth. Historically, Staffordshire was divided into five 'hundreds', under the rule of King Alfred the Great: Cuttlestone, Offlow, Pirehill, Seisdon, and Totmonslow. The historic boundaries of Staffordshire cover much of what is now the metropolitan county of West Midlands. An administrative county of Staffordshire was set up in 1889 under the Local Government Act 1888, covering the county except the county boroughs of Wolverhampton, Walsall, and West Bromwich in the south (the area known as the Black Country), and Hanley in the north. The legislation also saw the towns of Tamworth (partly in Warwickshire) and Burton-upon-Trent (partly in Derbyshire) united entirely in Staffordshire.

In 1553, Queen Mary made Lichfield a county corporate, meaning it was administered separately from the rest of Staffordshire. It remained so until 1888. Handsworth and Perry Barr became part of the county borough of Birmingham in the early twentieth century, and thus associated with Warwickshire. Burton, in the east of the county, became a county borough in 1901, and was followed by Smethwick, another town in the Black Country, in 1907. In 1910, the six towns of the Staffordshire Potteries, including Hanley, became the single county borough of Stoke-on-Trent. A significant boundary change occurred in 1926 when the east of Sedgley was transferred to Worcestershire to allow the construction of the new Priory Estate on land purchased by Dudley County Borough council.

A major reorganisation in the Black Country in 1966, under the recommendation of the Local Government Commission for England, led to the creation of an area of contiguous county boroughs. The County Borough of Warley was formed by the merger of the county borough of Smethwick and municipal borough of Rowley Regis with the Worcestershire borough of Oldbury; the resulting county borough was associated with Worcestershire. Meanwhile, the county borough of Dudley, historically a detached part of Worcestershire, expanded and became associated with Staffordshire instead. This reorganisation led to the administrative county of Staffordshire having a thin protrusion passing between the county boroughs (to the east) and Shropshire, to the west, to form a short border with Worcestershire.

Come spring of 1974, under the Local Government Act 1972, the county boroughs of the Black Country, along with the Aldridge-Brownhills Urban District of Staffordshire, found themselves swallowed whole by a new beast – the metropolitan county of West Midlands. The county boroughs were snuffed out, and Stoke was demoted to a non-metropolitan district in Staffordshire, and Burton formed an unparished area in the district of East Staffordshire. It would be more than two decades before the Banham Commission's decree breathed life back into Stoke-on-Trent, making it a unitary authority. Cut loose from Staffordshire's grip it was free to form a new identity, free, but forever haunted by the scars of its past.

Staffordshire's large market town and borough Tamworth is 14 miles (23 kilometers) north-east of Birmingham and 103 miles

(166 kilometers) north-west of London. Bordering Warwickshire to the south and east, and Lichfield to the north and west, Tamworth takes its name from the River Tame, which flows through it. This heritage-rich town is the home of the historic Tamworth Castle, the Church of St Editha and Moat House, and was the capital of the Anglo-Saxon Kingdom of Mercia. The town's main industries include logistics, engineering, clothing, brick, tile and paper manufacture.

Established in 1842, the Staffordshire Constabulary, as it was known, was the main police force for the county of Staffordshire. In the last two centuries it has gone through several name changes: Staffordshire Constabulary, 1842–1929; Staffordshire County Police, 1929–1967 and then from New Year's Day 1968 until 1974 its name reflected the amalgamation between Staffordshire County and its neighbouring city Stoke on Trent (and was named Staffordshire County & Stoke on Trent Constabulary) between 1968-1974 and thereafter became known as Staffordshire Police. The constabulary also had the Borough of Newcastle-under-Lyme Police, which became part of Staffordshire County Police in 1947, and City of Lichfield Police. Until the full amalgamation of the county in 1974, it was quite parochial.

Staffordshire Police was externally bordered by eight other county and borough police forces in 1972 (clockwise): Cheshire Police, Derbyshire Constabulary, Leicestershire Police, Warwickshire Police, West Midlands Police, Birmingham City Police, Worcester City Police and Shropshire Constabulary. When the constabulary became known as Staffordshire Police on 1 April 1974, it incorporated its other internal police forces.

Our story begins in Wigginton, a village in the district of Lichfield in Staffordshire, England. Its nearest town is Tamworth, lying about 2 miles (3 kilometers) to its north. The name 'Wigginton' is believed to come from Old English and means Wicga's farm. The name was also sometimes written as Wiggington. The village lies on a medieval trade route, the Portway, possibly used for transporting salt from the River Mease at Edingale to Tamworth.

Once, Wigginton was merely a chapelry, tethered to the parish of St. Editha in Tamworth. Civilly, it bore the title of a township, a label that stretched beyond the boundaries of the village itself, roping in the small hamlets of Comberford and Coton—though Coton has since been devoured by the ever-hungry borough of Tamworth. In 1866, it was reborn as a civil parish. By 1894, it was further encompassed by the sprawling Tamworth Rural District. And then, in 1934, the civil parish evolved once more, expanding its reach to encompass Wigginton and Hopwas, becoming a part of the Lichfield Rural District.

In 1861, the population of Wigginton township was 670 on 3,470 acres (1,400 hectares). This figure included eighty-four inmates of the Tamworth workhouse, which at that time lay within the township. The population of the chapelry alone was 466.

Its intense geographical history and stunning layout aside, Staffordshire has a sombre past. The stained pages of its history books are smudged and depressed by the tears of the townspeople who have cried over loved ones lost to a sin most foul: murder. Most notable were the killings of multiple young schoolgirls. The series of tragic events that occurred in the early to mid-1960s became known colloquially as the 'Cannock Chase murders' (also known as the 'A34 murders'). Starting in 1964, there was a wave of attempted abductions and attacks on young girls. The first suspected (but still unconfirmed) victim was 9-year-old Julia Taylor. A series of events played out that led to her attack, resembling the cautionary tale many are warned about as children. The young girl was lured into a car in Bloxwich on 1 December 1964 by a man claiming to be a friend of her mother. Julia was sexually assaulted, strangled, and left for dead in Bloxwich Lane. Her saviour came in the shape of a passing cyclist who spotted her body and raised the alarm and, as a result, stopped her from a prolonged exposure to the elements and death.

Just days after Julia's attack, newspapers reported that a new law would see the end of capital punishment in England:

> no person shall suffer death for murder and a person guilty of murder shall be sentenced to imprisonment for life.

Hanging was suspended as a form of punishment for murder before capital punishment was finally abolished in 1969 for all crimes except treason, which would continue for another twenty-nine years. It would be a move that came too early for one of Staffordshire's most notorious and dangerous serial killers. At first Julia's attack appeared to be a one-off incident, but barely a year later, on Wednesday, 8 September 1965, 6-year-old Margaret Reynolds went missing on her way to school in Aston, Birmingham. The young girl had left her home in Clifton Road at 1.45 pm with her older sister Susan. The girls had walked to the end of the street, hand in hand, before they released their grasps to go in opposite directions to their schools. When she failed to return home from school, the alarm was raised. Two thousand people searched for Margaret in the hours following her disappearance, but the search yielded no results. Police feared the girl had become trapped in and amongst Aston's mass of industrial premises. More than 100 police officers, equipped with the newest technology at the time, two-way radios, scoured the area, and newspapers reported daily, displaying the latest picture of the lost beaming bob-haired girl. Despite a frantic search, little was discovered about her whereabouts. With Margaret still missing, that same year on 30 December, 5-year-old Diana Joy Tift vanished as she walked to her grandmother's house in Bloxwich. Less than a fortnight later, the bodies of the two missing girls were found almost side by side in a ditch at Mansty Gully on Cannock Chase in Staffordshire.

Murder is a terrible act, but the murder of children is a destruction of nature's most innocent and gentle living things. The aftermath of the discovery sent shockwaves through the community. Staffordshire's people had barely recovered when another murder smashed through their grief. On a balmy August afternoon the following year, 7-year-old Christine Ann Darby was enticed into the car of a stranger near her home in Camden Street, Caldmore, Walsall. Her naked body was found three days later, beneath bracken, only 1 mile away from where Margaret Reynolds and Diana Tift had been discovered. She had been sexually assaulted. Speaking to local reporters about the nature of the person responsible for the death of the little girl, DCS Ian Forbes of New Scotland Yard told them:

> Any man who kidnaps and does away with a little girl like this is indeed dangerous.

Witnesses in Walsall recalled that on the day Christine Darby had disappeared they had seen a man in a grey car who spoke in a local accent. Two others who had been on Cannock Chase remembered seeing a grey Austin A55 or A60 car. Police were looking for a man with dark hair, aged 30 to 40, with a regional West Midlands accent.

The *modus operandi* of each of the murders was identical – each victim was thought to have been coaxed into a car while near her home, sexually assaulted, and then murdered. Julia, Margaret and Diana all lived within a 17-mile radius of each other and near the A34 road that passes through Cannock Chase.

At the time of the murders, the nation was still reeling in horror from the crimes of Ian Brady and Myra Hindley, a seemingly ordinary couple from Manchester who had been found guilty of abducting five children – Pauline Reade, John Kilbride, Keith Bennett, Lesley Ann Downey and Edward Evans – aged between 10 and 17. The evil pair sexually assaulted four of the children. Three bodies in total were discovered on Saddleworth Moor, 60 miles north of Staffordshire- two in 1965 and a further one in 1987, more than 20 years after their incarceration. One victim, Keith Bennett is believed to be lost out there still. But in the wake of this fresh wave of tragedy, a police investigation was launched, which was more intense and exhaustive than that of the infamous moors murders. The investigation into the murdered girls became one of the biggest in British criminal history. Prior to making an arrest, 150 detectives visited 39,000 homes, interviewed 80,000 people, and checked over 1 million car forms. Culling 25,000 vehicles from more than 1 million files, investigators checked every Austin A55 and A60 in the Midlands. Staffordshire's assistant chief constable at the time, Sir Stanley Bailey, spearheaded the operation to find the Cannock Chase murderer.

Technology had advanced at such a time that allowed, for the first time in British criminal history, for a facial composite sketch to be used, and though no one came forward to identify anyone on the basis of the image released, when police eventually arrested the perpetrator behind these heinous crimes, they were struck by his resemblance to the coloured identikit picture that they had circulated.

Technology is often no true match for good old-fashioned coppering though, and the killer's undoing came after the attempted abduction of 10-year-old Margaret Aulton on 4 November 1968 in Walsall. Like his victims before, the man with a West Midlands accent tried to force the little girl into his green and white Ford Corsair but she broke away. The incident was witnessed by Wendy Lane, a housewife who lived on Rollingmill Street, who made the quick decision to make a note of the vehicle registration plate after seeing it speed away. The police were called, who in turn called out the local vehicle registrations officer for Walsall. Margaret bravely gave a description of the car and the watch worn by her attacker. Police realised that the witness had mixed up two of the numbers from the registration she had remembered. After some rearranging of the numbers, police located a local record for a green and white Ford Corsair, which was registered to Raymond

Leslie Morris from Walsall. He was quickly arrested in connection with the attempted abduction.

The police were aware that Morris, who had been interviewed four times in four years in relation to the murders, had previously owned a grey Austin A55 similar to the one used in the abduction of Christine Darby. At the time of the investigation, he had been considered a suspect in her death, but his wife provided him with an alibi stating that the couple were shopping together the day Christine went missing. A police search of the Morris flat uncovered pornographic photographs of a child, later determined to be his wife's 5-year-old niece. New Scotland Yard detectives arrested Morris for Christine's murder on 16 November 1968. Two charges of indecent assault on his wife's niece and one for the attempted abduction of Margaret Aulton were also filed against Morris. The same year that Diana Tift and Margaret Reynolds had been found dead, 10-year-old Jane Taylor was abducted as she rode her bicycle through the village of Mobberley. Her body has never been found. Investigators could not disprove her disappearance was linked to the 'Cannock Chase murders'.

Morris was convicted of the murder of Christine Darby at Staffordshire Assizes on 19 February 1969, after one of the largest manhunts in British history. Christine's mother, Lillian Darby, sat at the front of the court as her daughter's killer was sentenced. Three rows behind her sat Morris's wife, who had provided him with the alibi. His parents were also in court. The judge commended the work of DCS Forbes of New Scotland Yard, who was reported to have not seen his own family for five months in the hunt for Christine's killer. The judge told Forbes after Morris was sentenced:

> The people of this county and I would have said the people of the whole country owe a debt of gratitude to you and those who have served you for what you have done.

There was not enough proof to determine if Morris was responsible for the 1965 murders of Diana Tiff and Margaret Reynolds, nor the earlier attack on Julia Taylor. However, as he sat in court for his murder trial, the surviving victim, Margaret Aulton, now a teenager, gazed upon Morris and recognised him immediately. Morris's condemnation would come in the damning words she cried as her gaze fell on the man in the dock:

That's him! That's the man who did it to me.

In 1971, a year before our story in Staffordshire begins, another Staffordshire mystery surfaced approximately 15 miles to the north of Wigginton in Winshill, Burton-on-Trent. On 27 March 1971, a young Staffordshire special constable named David Nathan was out walking his dog when he stumbled across what he thought was a bag of cement on a river island off Newton Road, but a closer look suggested this to be something of a much more ominous find. The off-duty officer immediately notified Burton Police of his discovery. A digging operation, led by Chief Superintendent Raymond Felgate, was launched. Upon further inspection, that bag of 'cement' was discovered to be a body. The victim, a male, had been buried in a kneeling position – his hands and ankles had been bound.

Forensic testing deemed the male to be aged between 24 and 36. A Caucasian European, he once stood at 172 centimeters tall, and was of thin build. It is believed he had been there for nine to twelve months. He had a partial upper denture and had extensive dental work done less than six months before his death. His hair had been brown, straight and short, no more than 3 inches in length. The victim was considered to have had a neck condition, which would cause his head to lean to the right. Strangely unique to this case, the victim was naked except for pink socks and a wedding ring. Despite numerous television appeals, a painstaking reconstruction of the man's head and even a book, the victim remains unknown. The locals referred to this mystery as 'Fred the Head'. His killer (or killers) possibly still walks the streets.

The location of the body gave police cause for concern – today, it is 100 yards from the busy Newton Road. However, in previous decades there were only two routes to the spot, which was once the site of a flint mill. One path to the area was across a bridge that was gated and locked on both sides. Given the secure nature of that route, it is unlikely the killer(s) used that walkway. The other route was across Burton Bridge, along a rough track and through fields – a much more public and accessible route. Police theorised that the killer (or killers) was local and knew the area well.

In 2017, detectives hit a fresh roadblock in the long search for answers. 'Fred the Head' was given a face by Professor Caroline Wilkinson, an expert in facial reconstruction at the University of Liverpool who, in the past, has reconstructed the features of Richard III, Robert the Bruce and even Father Christmas. Police admitted that the dead man was not an individual listed as missing from Llangollen in November 1970. In 2018, BBC's appeals programme *Crimewatch Roadshow* revisited the case prompting a family from Cardiff to come forward to Staffordshire Police claiming that the man was John Henry Jones, but familial DNA testing has proved this to not be the case, ruling out the force's most promising lead. To this day, detectives still hope a family member will step from the shadows and name the victim.

Staffordshire's history of brutal crimes is merely a charred piece on a rich and colourful mosaic of its heritage, but the idea that one of the most dangerous and deranged killers in British history could have come to town with murder in mind could reveal a very different picture.

Chapter Two

A Murder Most Foul

With Morris behind bars, the county of Staffordshire could begin to heal from these most tragic of events. But alas, it would be only four years before tragedy struck once again. Tamworth's Comberford Lane runs westwards for 2 miles from the pretty village of Wigginton, through open fields of luscious fertile soil and onto the main A513 road out of the Staffordshire market town, home to the founder of the modern police force, Sir Robert Peel. One might be familiar with the common policeman noun of 'Bobbies' when referring to police or, as they were called once upon a time, 'Peelers'. Exposed and rural Comberford Lane, Wigginton in 1972 was popular with what newspapers euphemistically term 'courting couples'. This 'lovers' lane' dissects the A513 road to the west of the village and what used to be the A453 Ashby Road to the east (since built as the A42/M42); the latter leading via Ashby-de-la-Zouch to Kegworth and the M1 motorway.

The Met Office recorded that in 1972, England experienced more than 1,300 hours of sunshine in the entire year. Summer 1972 was an especially hot one. So scorching was the summer heat that local police would head to the local outdoor swimming pools to cool off between their shifts. At around 6.00 pm on Wednesday, 7 June 1972, a 14-year-old grammar school student by the name of Judith Roberts stormed out of the gates of 155 Gillway Lane, Wigginton – the home she shared with her parents Vincent and Julia, and three siblings, Ann, Rebecca and Nicola. The young girl was a student at the nearby Queen Elizabeth Grammar School in Tamworth, where her father was head of physical education and Bernard Baker was the headmaster. As well as a sister, she was a non-identical twin to Ann and known as a shy, timid third form pupil by her peers in form 3G, where she had a small group of friends. Judith was also of an age that allowed her to be a cadet with the Tamworth's Red Cross detachment and she enjoyed dancing with her friends at Mollie Parkes School of Dancing.

As the evening was drawing in, Judith mounted her traditional green Raleigh bicycle, which had been a present from her parents two years earlier, and began to cycle up Main Road, then along Comberford Lane, which continues west until the point where it becomes Wigginton Lane. Judith often took this route. Just as it did back then, today the area sits astride multiple rolling fields.

According to the details her parents gave to police in the aftermath of her disappearance, Judith's normal routine was that she would arrive home from school at around 4.30 pm, have tea, and then complete about one hour of homework before going for a ride on her bicycle. She would cycle 'round the block' – encompassing Gillway Lane, Wigginton Road, Comberford Lane and Comberford Road – then back to Gillway Lane and home. On occasions she would call at Borough Road Post Office and Sweet Shop, which closed at 6.00 pm. On these occasions Judith would leave Borough Road, cycling into Lakenheath Road in Mildenhall and then back onto Wigginton Road to complete the circuit.

On this particular day, Wednesday, 7 June 1972, her routine was just as it was every other day. She arrived home at around 4.30 pm after her school day had finished. Her mother, Julia, had prepared a salad and banana custard for tea, but Judith didn't feel like eating. Judith's mother recalled that her daughter was growing concerned that she was fat following 'someone making silly remarks'. Her parents' attempts to soothe her worries fell on deaf ears. Judith left her salad but begrudgingly swallowed down the banana custard and a drink. Her mother warned Judith that she would tell her father that she was not eating, but despite the threat of her father's disapproving tongue, Judith refused to relent. At around 5.15 pm her father arrived home from work to find that instead of having her tea, Judith was hunched over her homework in the living room, thoroughly engrossed, having missed tea with her mother and siblings. Vincent called his daughter in from the living room and asked her to join him at the kitchen table. Before her father, Judith meekly nibbled at some lettuce, a tomato and a spring onion. Growing frustrated at his daughter, Vincent scolded Judith for not eating her food and instructed her to finish her homework, telling her she would eat what food she had left for her supper. Judith walked back into the living room, where she finished her homework before standing up and collecting her navy-blue anorak and walked to the shed in the back garden. There, she let her pet hamster, Horace, out of his cage and left a notice on the shed door to the effect of 'Horace on the floor' and left on her cycle. Judith was still dressed in her school clothes: a blue and white dress, her navy-blue anorak and black lace-up shoes. Underneath her school clothes she wore a bra and two pairs of pants (one under a pair of fawn-coloured tights, the other over).

Judith's neighbour, Bertha Evans, of 153 Gillway Lane would later tell detectives how she saw Judith go left out of number 155 onto Gillway Lane in the direction of Wigginton Road that evening. Maude Best of 134 Gillway Lane, who was out walking her dog, would later say she had seen Judith near the junction with Wigginton Road and Brown's Lane. Judith stopped briefly for a quick conversation with her neighbour before pedaling off. Judith would normally be back by around 8.00 pm to watch *Crossroads*, a popular Midlands-based teatime soap opera of the era, but she wouldn't make it home that night. At around 7.00 pm Judith came to Comerford Lane, where it is suspected she became separated from her cycle for reasons unknown. A pathologist report suggests that around this time, she was subjected to a frenzied attack.

Judith's parents were worried when she didn't return at her usual time, and as 10.00 pm came and passed, their concern had grown beyond frantic as to their daughter's whereabouts. By now, the summer sun had stopped shining and the skies were black outside. Vincent did a search of the house and gardens, to check she had not returned, before taking a torch out around the area to see if he could spot her. With no sign of Judith and with the day growing to a close, at 10.30 pm he felt he had no choice but to inform the police that his daughter was missing.

A police investigation immediately sprang into action and an intensive search of the area was launched. When a child goes missing, police must act fast if they are to have any hope of finding them alive. This is now known as the 'Golden Hour' Principle in policing, and refers to the first 48 hours after someone is missing and the evidence, forensic or otherwise that can be amassed. The College of Policing cites that: 'The golden hour principle will also apply to the discovery of any new scene, arrest of suspect or other key activity that has a time-critical implication – for example, CCTV opportunities'. Cameras were not a consideration in 1972, and neither, officially, was the Golden Hour Principle, but no force knew to act as fast as Staffordshire Police, having only recently put to bed the tragedy that was the 'Cannock Chase murders' three years earlier. Police with dogs spread out across the town helped by civilian volunteers, a mountain rescue team, as well as RAF airmen and troops from Whittington Barracks. A description of Judith was widely distributed: standing at only 5 feet and 1 inch tall, she was described as a girl of medium build, with fair skin and hair, a half fringe and brace on her upper front teeth. The search for Judith continued through the whole of Thursday. By Friday, police and tracker dogs were scouring canals, rivers, pools and nearby farm buildings, but still no sight of Judith. Taxi drivers and bus crews were asked to be on the lookout for the missing schoolgirl.

Despite the unusually hot weather that summer 1972 had displayed, Saturday, 10 June 1972 was a wet and rainy day, mirroring the sombre atmosphere of a town stricken by tragedy. On this morning, the tabloid newspaper *Birmingham Evening Mail*, printed a story that carried with it photographs which revealed the concerned faces of Judith's parents. Distributed around Birmingham where it was based, as well as its neighbouring county, the Black Country, the newspaper was also a prominent news source for the residents of Solihull, parts of Warwickshire, Worcestershire and Staffordshire. It quoted Judith's mother's desperate pleas for her daughter to 'come home, all is forgiven'. She had told reporters she felt that perhaps a friend was sheltering her daughter, providing her with food and a place to rest in the aftermath of the tiff between them. 'Judith is such a timid girl, she would never stay out late,' the young girl's mother told *Birmingham Evening Mail* reporters, adding:

> I could not imagine that she would go to any strange place or with a stranger. I think she must be with a friend somewhere.

Some twins claim to have what is known as 'twin telepathy', the ability to know the thoughts and feelings of their sibling who they shared a womb with for nine months before being separated at birth. Ann told reporters:

> Normally we think alike, but I can't imagine what has happened.

On this same morning, approximately 300 troops from the nearby Whittington Barracks, police, civilians and dogs were on call in the search for Judith. The entire junior soldiers' company stationed at Whittington Barracks in Lichfield was taken to attend a search of fields to the west of Wiggington Road, which adjoined Comberford Lane. Part of that search team was 16-year-old Private Barrie Keith Gibson from Wolverhampton. Also part of the search team was Lance

Corporal Trevor George Steele, a soldier in the Cheshire Regiment from Crewe, who was also stationed at Whittington Barracks. According to a statement made by Gibson, it was at around 2.30 pm that afternoon that the team commenced searching fields from south to north on the western side of Wigginton Village and Wigginton Road; there was still no sign of Judith.

At about 4.30 pm, the search came to a local corn field known as Robinson's Field, not far from a gated entrance behind a 12-foot-high hedge in Comberford Lane. In his police statement, Gibson wrote:

> On reaching Comberford Lane we commenced searching the field on the other side of the lane. To enter this field, which had been roughly ploughed, I opened a gate and walked in first in front of L/Cpl Steele.

Gibson says he went in first, followed closely by Steele who was about 7 yards behind him. Within minutes of entering the field, Gibson made the first of three horrific discoveries: the private spotted a green bicycle laying still in an overgrown thorn hedge, approximately 16 feet from the field gate on the north side of Comberford Lane. The front wheel was protruding from the shrubbery facing towards the gate. Gibson wrote:

> [I] turned left and started to walk up the hedge ... I had gone about seven yards when I saw about two yards in front of me a green Moulton pedal cycle lying into the hedge with the front wheel towards the gate. I shouted and was joined at once by L/Cpl Steele and others.

Hearing the alarming cries of his comrade, Steele joined Gibson and the pair continued to scour the hedgerow, with Gibson still ahead of him. As their eyes scanned the overgrown sides of Robinson's Field, the junior soldier passed by a pile of leaves, but Steele's eyes rested firmly on something strange in the foliage.

> I noticed about a yard to the right of the cycle a mound of hedge cuttings.

As Steele's eyes focused on the inconspicuous mound of shrubbery, something else caught his eye.

> At the same time I noticed a piece of blue coloured material sticking out from the mound of hedge cuttings. I then went across to this mound. I saw that this mound consisted of twigs and privet hedge cuttings. I then lifted the blue piece of cloth with my right hand and saw human hair covered with blood and I saw a piece of human flesh.

A horrified Gibson said:

> As soon as I saw this I moved away from the scene.

The third and final tragic discovery came soon after. Underneath the hedge cuttings were three pieces of corrugated asbestos, concealing two fertiliser bags. Beneath these, Judith's lifeless body lay, face down. Further forensic investigations would soon reveal she had been bludgeoned to death, her skull shattered into eighteen fragments before she was committed to a crude shallow grave in the field, pushed feet first under the hedge; In a sad and twisted coincidence, the field could just about be seen from Judith's bedroom window back in Gillway Lane, less than 1 mile away. Unbeknown to Steele at the time, the blue material he held in his hand had been the blue anorak that Judith donned before she set off on her cycle just three days earlier.

Luminous flares were sent up into the gloomy sky to guide officers to the scene. Staffordshire Police were at the scene within minutes of receiving the call to alert them a body had been found during the search for the missing schoolgirl.

The team of police officers who look after such high-profile cases often fall to much scrutiny; they are in a race to find the answers to questions that are light years beyond their scope thanks to things like forensic science. Things we now take for granted such as CCTV surveillance and fingerprint evidence were a thing of the future at this time, not that it bothered a man like DCS Wright, the head of Staffordshire and Stoke-on-Trent CID. He would be described by his son Ian Wright (after his death in March 2018 at the age of 98) to reporters from *The Sentinel* as a man who used 'old-fashioned policing' to crack cases. Having worked his way through the ranks from superintendent in Leek to divisional commander in Stafford, DCS Wright had headed Staffordshire and Stoke-on-Trent CID for almost a decade, but one of his most infamous cases was currently brewing. In the north-west of England, Donald Neilson was working his way through what would be eighteen armed robberies and eventually, a spate of murders, culminating in the 1975 murder of coach heiress Lesley Whittle from Shropshire. Her emaciated body was found hanging inside a drain in Kidsgrove Bathpool Park after an intense search for her following messages from Neilson demanding ransom for her safe return. Wright ensured that Neilson was brought to justice, securing an eighteen-page confession by the killer. According to those who were closest to Wright, he lived and breathed his cases before eventually retiring in 1977.

Also part of the team investigating Judith's case was Chief Constable Arthur Rees of Staffordshire Police, a well-respected commander of his peers. Ever since his days as an acting wing commander during the Second World War, the Welsh-born pilot led an interesting life. According to an obituary in *The Independent* after his death on 13 May 1998, Rees's career with the police began in 1935 when he joined the Metropolitan Police force.

> He resumed his service with the Met after the war, climbing the ranks over the next 11 years before taking over as Chief Constable of Denbighshire in 1957. He spent six years in his native Wales before moving back to England to take over as Chief Constable of Staffordshire. He held that post between 1964–67 before assuming the new title of Chief Constable of Staffordshire and Stoke-on-Trent between 1968 and his retirement in 1977. As well as playing Rugby for Cambridge University, the RAF, the Metropolitan Police, Surrey and the Barbarians, Rees was also a stalwart of London Welsh and Crawshay's Welsh RFC, where he served as Chairman 1960–92 and President from 1992.

Chief Constable Rees's assistant chief constable was Harry A. Bailey. Years before, during the 'Cannock Chase murders', Bailey had been the detective chief superintendent on the case. DSI Frank Jordan, who had confirmed to reporters the discovery of the remains of 'Fred the Head' in 1971, and DC Ephraim Prince. were just some of the detectives who came to Robinson's Field that Saturday afternoon.

The Home Office pathologist, Dr Scholtz Barendo van der Merwe, was summoned to the location, given a police escort from his home on the outskirts of Derbyshire, and arrived approximately two hours later. Dr van der Merwe had been born in South Africa in 1916. He moved to England after he spent one year studying medicine in his native country. By 1951, he had been appointed a consultant pathologist in Burton-on-Trent. The towns and villages of Lichfield, Tamworth and Sutton Coldfield also fell under his jurisdiction. Described in his obituary as 'one of the last generalists'. He had been a Home Office pathologist since 1959. In his report on the scene DCS Wright wrote:

At 4:35pm on Saturday 10th June 1972 I visited a field off Comberford Lane, Tamworth with the Assistant Chief Constable (Crime) Mr H.A. Bailey. I saw that the field appeared to have been roughly ploughed, also that there was a fairly wide border of rough ground over which grass and weeds were growing, reasonably short near to the ploughed side, but very long under the overhanging hedge, which was running parallel to Comberford Lane. I also saw a new looking green coloured pedal cycle ... Lying in the foot of the hedge some sixteen feet from the gateway ... and noticed that it was not visible until I had walked a distance of several yards into the field. Bits of rubbish and pieces of brick lay on the grass verge and a pile of privet hedge cuttings lay inside the field to the left front of the gateway ... A second pile of privet hedge cuttings lay further away from the gateway, below the overhanging hedge and protruding from this I saw what appeared to be part of a blue-coloured anorak, a corner of white plastic material and a human hand ... At 6:45pm the same day I was present when Doctor Van-der-Merwe explored the second pile of hedge cuttings and saw the Doctor hand to Detective Constable Prince:- A quantity of privet hedge cuttings removed from the top of the body; three pieces of corrugated asbestos sheeting from the top of the body; a blue plastic bag off the top of the body; a white plastic bag off the top of the body; a piece of line post from the right side of the body; a pair of pants and tights from against the left hip; a pair of pants from against the right hip; a left shoe from against the left hip; a right shoe from against the right hip. Both shoes were still laced and all the articles referred to above had been neatly placed on top or at the side of the body of the girl, which was lying face downwards. Judith's clothes had been tampered with and adjusted in a way that possibly suggested a sexual motive.

Judith's body was removed from the site and taken to the public mortuary in Kettlebrook. In what is a cruel but necessary formality, her father was called in to identify her. It is an impossible task that unfortunately too many parents are forced to do and comes with a heart wrenching catch-22: a positive identification eliminates hope of their child coming home alive, a negative result, however, prolongs the agony that comes with having no answers as to where they could be. But, for the Roberts family, three days of searching for Judith had surmounted to a devastating result, and any hopes that their beloved Judith could be found alive were devastatingly dashed.

Chapter Three

The Mark of a Serial Killer

Judith's body had only been inside the mortuary a couple of hours when Dr van der Merwe began the postmortem at 8.15 pm. DCS Wright was present when the examination on the body was carried out and watched Dr van der Merwe remove the remaining clothing that clung to Judith's body. Her navy-blue quilted pattern anorak was bloodstained in its upper part but not obviously torn, her checkered dress with a knotted belt pulled up over the chest at back and front, and a bra, which Dr van der Merwe described as 'intact and in place'. Working away methodically, dutifully and carefully, Dr van der Merwe would have noticed the multiple injuries to the left side of Judith's face, temple and scalp, but the true extent of her injuries was still to be documented. It would be a further ten days before a full examination of Judith's body would take place.

In the meantime, the investigation into who killed Judith ramped up. The following day more than seventy detectives combed Robinson's Field for clues and made door to door enquiries throughout Tamworth. Meanwhile, regional and national newspapers delivered the devastating details of the young girl from Tamworth who had been murdered on her daily bicycle ride. Page nine of the *Daily Express* reported just two days after her body was discovered that:

> [the] quiet and timid 14-year-old had been teased by schoolmates about her weight and so she had started dieting – possibly explaining further her reluctance to finish her tea the day she was last seen alive.

Reporters dissected the details of the family tiff that had 'led her to a terrible fate at the hands of a murderer' on the lonely 'lovers' lane' that dreadful summer's evening. But newspapers hardly needed to elaborate on the awful fate of young Judith. On 12th June 1972 an Express reporter wrote:

> A man dragged Judith into a cornfield, sexually assaulted her and battered her to death.

On Wednesday, 14 June 1972, Judith's twin sister, Ann, embarked on a brave and difficult journey: as the twin sister of Judith, police hoped that her figure, riding Judith's bicycle dressed in her uniform might jog the memory of some of the local people and force them to recall important details about the evening she vanished. Wearing a blue and white school uniform dress and a blue anorak, Ann rode Judith's green bicycle back across the route her sister had last taken. The journey took place exactly a week to the minute that Judith was last seen. Scotland Yard detectives accompanied her on her ride along the 2-mile route. DCS Donald Saunders told reporters:

> We hope this might throw forward some vital clue ... some vital sighting of Judith on the night she died.

Of Ann's assistance he praised her assistance and her,

> great presence of mind and great determination.

Judith's mother told the *Sunday Mercury* reporters of her daughter's mood the last evening she had seen her alive:

> Judith started to go without food and we told her not to be silly as there was nothing wrong with her figure. But she would not

eat her tea and she stormed out saying she was going for a ride on her bike. She has done this before but always came back in about half an hour as if nothing had happened.

One thing was clear from the report, police were keen to find out quickly who had killed young Judith. The papers said detectives with billhooks were searching hedgerows trying to find the murder weapon. One senior officer said to the journalist:

> This is a particularly nasty murder ... Judith was certainly not a precocious girl, rather the reverse. She was not the sort to talk to strangers.

The investigation was plagued further when a letter – compiled with newspaper headlines reading 'Lichfield Schoolgirl dies next ... at weekend' – was received by police. The letter, with a Walsall, Staffordshire postmark, was delivered to a newspaper office on 15 June 1972 and was signed by the 'Tamworth Murderer'. The threat of Judith's murder potentially being repeated caused great concern for New Scotland Yard's DCS Saunders, who had been drafted into the murder investigation, and had warned parents to keep a firm eye on their children until the killer was caught. Nothing came of the threats in the letter and the person who 'penned' it remained anonymous, their identity never discovered, but fear was rife in the quiet Staffordshire town.

At 3.15 pm on Tuesday, 20 June 1972, DCS Saunders, DC Prince and DCS Wright attended the mortuary while Dr van der Merwe carried out a full examination of Judith's injuries. The Home Office pathologist had already made a note of the scene as he found it when he arrived at Robinson's Field the previous week. He had written in his report how the rain that had plagued Tamworth that day had still been falling when Judith's body was found; how the edges of the fields where her body had been discarded were fringed by long grass and weeds, while the remainder of the roughly ploughed field was short in comparison. As had been noted by DC Wright in his report, Dr van der Merwe made comments on the various pieces of rubbish and brick that had lay in the grass verge, the fresh privet hedge clippings and a pile of soil. He noted how further along the foot of the hedge and below its overhang, another pile of clippings was visible through a gap in the weeds and grass. The pathologist wrote about the scene, which he found in the field:

> This almost totally obscured the body of which only a hand was visible.

He continued:

> The grass beneath the body was flattened by the weight of the body, relatively orderly in fashion, not churned about and dry to the touch. The feet were extended well into the hedge with stems of dry grass and twigs caught between some toes. The site where the body lay was relatively orderly and gave the appearance that it had been placed there fairly carefully and that it had been pushed under the hedge feet first.

Dr van der Merwe wrote:

> This was a healthy girl of about 14 years of relatively slight build who died soon after severe blows to the left side of her head. She had been dead for approximately three days, lying under the north side of a thick hedge. The freshness of the vegetable fragments in her stomach indicated that she had these to eat some one or two hours prior to her death.

The most notable discovery of the postmortem was that Judith's skull had been fractured into eighteen pieces. He concluded that the young girl was struck multiple times while lying prone on the ground, face down, before the killer removed her shoes and tampered with the lower half of her clothing. Due to the position of her clothes, he summarised that there was an obvious sign of a sexual motive but there was no evidence that she had been raped.

In filling out his report, Dr van der Merwe compiled a catalogue of devastating injuries that were inflicted upon Judith:

> There were multiple injuries to the left side of the face, temple and scalp, and blood was present in the hair, had issued from both ears particularly the left and had flowed from the left side to the right which was more blood-stained. The hands were clenched, the left particularly blood-stained and with some bruising of the backs of the fingers and a loose fresh flap of skin on the index finger. Fine long hairs were caught up between the fingers. The right hand was slightly blood-stained only, and the nails of either hand were injured. The trunk showed a scrape mark, soil-stained, more on the left side of the waist and lower chest ending fairly abruptly at the line where the dress was pulled up and similarly stained.

He later stated that:

> In my opinion the earliest of the blows was a downward impact from her left side to the back of the head causing a crushing type laceration of the scalp, extending forward as a slicing injury by a relatively sharp-edged implement of some weight. It caused a depressed fracture of the back part of the skull where it is thickest and must have rendered her unconscious immediately, and would have been, inevitably, fatal.

Although Dr van der Merwe's notes are meticulous and consistent with the style in which a pathologist might record a postmortem in the 1970s, we couldn't help but ask what comments he might give today about his earlier report, given the advancement of technology and techniques in the fifty years since Judith's murder. Dr van der Merwe died in May 1994 after a long and distinguished career, and therefore the option to quiz him on his findings and experiences is, unfortunately, long lost. Looking to understand the jargon more thoroughly we interviewed Dr Stuart Hamilton, a Home Office registered forensic pathologist who covers the neighbouring area, the East Midlands (Leicestershire, Northamptonshire, Lincolnshire, Nottinghamshire and Derbyshire). He has been a Home Office pathologist for more than a decade, a similar vantage point of the late Dr van der Merwe who at the time of Judith's murder had been a Home Office pathologist for thirteen years. Dr Hamilton's work was initially carried out in the north-east of England but he is now based in the Midlands. He tells us:

> These days we [the pathologists] would probably be very hands off in that aspect of it ... So, you'd have [at the murder scene] your forensic biologist, your crime scene investigators, all those people would be doing the scene and we would very much step back from that. In fact, with the increasing sensitivity of DNA technologies it's often better that we're not there because it's one less person to contaminate it.

He reminds us:

> This is not *Midsomer Murders* where you rock up and tell them everything they need to know in ten seconds.

When asked about his initial thoughts on the pathology report he had some interesting insights. He told us:

> My initial impression is that she's been hit on the head with a hammer and it was sexually motivated.

Dr Hamilton also took time to reflect on the attitudes of forensic professionals in the early 1970s, attitudes that until the twenty-first century remained intact:

> The very strange thing about our job is that if you're talking about 50 years ago, we were probably less certain about everything than they would have been then because we're more willing now to accept biology has a lot of variables. I think in that era, maybe even professionals were a bit more naive, a little less worldly wise than maybe we are now.

He revealed to us:

> I've got a textbook from 2004, in which it says: 'It is no longer safe to assume that a woman with a tattoo is a prostitute.' That very old-fashioned attitude was very prevalent.

Looking over Dr van der Merwe's report, Dr Hamilton said:

> It struck me immediately that obviously the position of the clothing is something that will grab your attention straight away and clothing lifted up, particularly on a young woman, there's one thing that immediately leaps to mind, but equally if we've got somebody who has been dragged and placed obviously clothing can ride up if you're being dragged, so it

would be something that I would be interested in, but not placing too much weight on at that point.

Examining Judith's skull on 20 June 1972, Dr van der Merwe's report reads:

> A depression impression in this area was caused by a brick on which that part of the body lay. A similar scrape mark of soil was present on the inner back side of the left upper arm, deeply demarcated by the edge of the short sleeve dress. Two faint circular bruises were present on the inner side of the right upper arm, each approximately an inch in size.

One of his most shocking revelations would follow:

> On the skin of the lower abdomen a faintly glistening, irregular, whitish series of marks or tracks were present ...

Dr Hamilton almost immediately drew our attention to this detail of the report:

> I am interested in this 'snail trail' on her abdomen – that's got a huge question mark over it. It doesn't seem to have particularly raised any flags from what I can see but for me it's the sort of thing that sadly my brain says 'Yes'. I'd be sticking a swab in that, scraping some off and finding out what the heck it was ... it never occurred to them that this could be the unpleasantness that it is.

Could this section of the pathologist's report suggest that Judith was dragged by her upper right arm from the first attack scene on

Comberford Lane to the second in Robinson's Field where her body was further violated? It seems that way, although at the trial of the man accused of killing Judith the following year, Dr van der Merwe would say Judith didn't appear to have been dragged.

Dr van der Merwe's report continues to detail the extent of the injuries to Judith's scalp and face:

> Superficial abrasion and bruising on the bridge of the nose, a curved superficial abrasion and bruising on the bridge of the nose, a curved superficial laceration on the left cheekbone [*sic*] and an abrasion between it and the ear lobe. A curved superficial abrasion at the outer corner of the left eye. A penetrating laceration of the scalp above the left eyebrow 2 cm long and a roughly parallel series of five penetrating lacerations from the corner of the left eyebrow, extending towards the middle of the side of the head above the ear. They measured approximately 1 cm–2 cm long and were either linear, with neat edges, slightly sliced or with a rectangular shape due to gaping. Above these, and near the vertex was a further penetrating laceration, linear shaped, with ragged edges 2 cm long. A neat slicing laceration 10–11 cm long, curved over the back of the left side of the scalp exposing the skull. At the back end of this laceration, it was more ragged and had a more crushed appearance. Extensive haemorrhage had occurred deep to these left-sided lacerations and was caused by extensive depressed fractures of the skull. At the back end of the long laceration was a superficial 1cm long laceration which had not bled. Over the occiput were a group of three vertical lacerations 2–2.5cm long, like the rest neat slightly shelving or slicing. No haemorrhage was apparent from these …

How can we best distinguish what caused these marks on Judith's face and scalp? Dr Hamilton breaks it down for us:

> Certainly, nowadays there is very, very precise terminology in describing injuries. So, for a forensic pathologist now a 'laceration' is an injury caused by blunt trauma. So, if somebody gets punched in the face and splits their eyebrow, that is a laceration. If it is cut with a sharp object such as a knife, then it is an incised wound. I'm not one hundred percent clear quite how precisely the terminology is being used because he describes a 'neat slicing laceration ten to eleven centimeters long' so that suggests that he's talking about something incised but he's described it as a laceration. I think probably more helpful in this instance is to look at the photographs that we have and they look, I would describe them, as intermediate between a laceration and in incised wounds, so they're a bit ragged, they've got quite rough edges but they're quite regularly sized and shaped as well, so I think it looks like something that is sharp-ish or got a corner or an edge to it, but not something as sharp as a knife.

We can't help but wonder, was Judith's killer disturbed in the middle of their attack? If so, could this have prompted them to hurriedly hide both the body and bicycle, using materials found nearby?

The pathologist's report is interpreted by us to show that Judith, at the time of the initial attack, had dismounted and was walking down Comberford Lane close to the entrance to Robinson's Field, wheeling her bicycle to her right and probably engaged in conversation with her attacker, who had diverted her from cycling and was walking to her left, slightly behind. Judith was then delivered one almighty blow by a right-handed person from a heavy, narrow-edged metal object.

Our supposition and theory being that the injury was sustained at the narrow end of a horizontal 'walling hammer'. This would fit Dr van der Merwe's description of the weapon in his report of 'a relatively sharp-edged implement of some weight'.

Dr Hamilton is no stranger to homicide, and throughout his years he has seen a vast array of instruments used to kill. We had our own suspicions about the type of weapon used, which was not previously revealed to Dr Hamilton, but were echoed in his sentiments:

> I've seen a few people who've been stabbed in the head and with a typical knife you can leave the tip in the skull from it breaking, but you need a bit of mass to actually fracture something. What it looks most like from the things that I've seen is something like a masonry hammer so a hammer with a square end so it's got a corner but it's got mass behind it.

When we discussed the theory that the weapon used to kill Judith could have been a walling hammer, Dr Hamilton replied:

> I think it's fair to say, if this was my case and the police brought me a walling hammer, I would be quite comfortable to say yes, that is more than capable of causing these injuries.

Our own theories aside, it is clear to see that Judith had been beaten to death by being struck with one massive blow to the head. Dr van der Merwe's report concluded that this heavy blow, which was dealt to the back of her head, was so severe that it fractured her skull and damaged her brain; it would have had the desired effect of knocking her to the ground, rendering her immediately unconscious. Death would have followed very quickly.

Dr van der Merwe's report read:

> The skull on the left side had very depressed and extensive and fragmented fractures involving the left temporal, parietal and, partly, occipital bones into which the fracture radiated.

He continued:

> On one intact part of the left parietal bone, deep to the long-curved laceration, was a superficial, inch broad, series of parallel scratch marks, each approximately 1/4 inch long on the bony surface. The maximum depressed part was below the posterior end of the long-curved laceration over the left ear and the most fragmented part was over the area of the left temple, underlying the series of parallel lacerations in the left temporal scalp. The fracture of the left side radiating downwards into the base of the skull, across it, through the middle fossa to the other side.

One notable comment made in page five of the report was that above Judith's right ear was a mark:

> a contiguous group of two, in the shape of a letter 'Y', neat edged, slicing and approximately four-centimetre overall length. No gross haemorrhage had occurred from this injury. Other than these there were no injuries on the right side of the head.

Again, there were discussions over what might have caused this important 'Y' mark which potentially links Judith to multiple other victims, all attacked/killed by one man, who we will discuss later on. Dr Hamilton told us:

> so, there are two hemorrhages having occurred from this injury, so the two explanations for that is coincidentally you've got two impacts next to each other that have formed a 'Y' shape or that you've got an impact from something that has that sort of configuration and has produced it.

We suspect it might be the latter, and that the 1.5-inch mark on Judith's scalp could be caused by a large Phillips screwdriver. Dr Hamilton continued:

> It's quite big but equally what we have to bear in mind is the scalp is quite a firm tissue as why it bleeds so much if you fracture it so it can certainly tear a bit bigger. I wouldn't immediately leap to a screwdriver for that I have to be utterly honest but I'd need better close up scaled photographs to give a definitive opinion. The phrase 'a screwdriver' is rather like saying 'a knife' so you know there's all types of varieties.

Dr Hamilton does go on to say that the injury could be interpreted in different ways and without being present at the postmortem it is hard to distinguish certain facts from photographs and reports alone.

> I'm happy with that assessment that we're not going too outlandish, you know if we say it could be a Phillips screwdriver nobody is going to go 'well that's absolutely ridiculous of course it's not a Phillips screwdriver.'

Dr van der Merwe concluded that the cause of death of Judith Roberts was a fractured skull, due to blows to the head with a sharp or potentially pointed object. He commented that:

At some stage she was dragged face downwards across soil leaving a grazed imprint of it on the left side of her abdomen, lower chest and left arm and was deposited feet first under the overhang of the hedge so that the left side of her face was uppermost. It is probable that it was in this position that the series of parallel stabbing type injuries were inflicted on the left temple area fragmenting the underlying bone.

Dr Hamilton's assessment of Dr van der Merwe's report and recording of Judith's manner of death was that:

It's a sustained assault to the head, which in itself, is difficult to imagine it is anything other than an intent to kill. So repeated blows to the head, what you are thinking about it that this is a murder not a robbery gone wrong so I think death was the most likely intention of the person doing it.

Surviving ITN footage shows that Staffordshire police officers spent considerable time and effort in clearing verges and drainage ditches along Comberford Lane. They were trying to locate discarded weapons but there was nothing at the scene that could have caused the massive head injury or the 'Y' mark. It was only some months later after the arrest of Andrew Evans that the police and Dr van der Merwe came up with the concept that the sheets of corrugated asbestos caused both the massive head fractures and the facial injuries, a theory which at best is fanciful and downright farcical at worst. Dr Hamilton told us:

I don't like the idea of a sheet of anything to cause these [injuries] to be honest with you.

Dr Hamilton continued:

It's not an effective weapon – people use things that are effective. If you're going to grab a fourteen-year-old girl and attack them, a sheet of asbestos, a sheet of anything, it's weight, it's difficult to get the weight, it's difficult to get mass. What I have to explain a lot of times in court is that objects are designed with a purpose, there is a reason why a filleting knife and a machete knife are different, because they are for different purposes and if you want to bash somebody's head in with a hammer is an obvious thing to do it with or you know a heavy screwdriver, but a sheet of corrugated stuff is not an effective weapon, it's certainly not given the severity of the injuries this young lady has.

Dr Hamilton's assessment of the report also picked up on Judith's lack of defence wounds:

She's got nothing defensive on her so whatever has happened to her, she has been overcome very quickly and has not responded to her assailant, she has been dragged.

But what of the killer who absconded from the scene? Dr Hamilton explained:

I would expect them [the killer] at very least to have fine splatter on them so as that hammer is going down, I say hammer, I think it's a hammer, the weapon, the implement, as it's striking, the blood is going to be jetting out in every direction. The harder you hit, the smaller the droplets so I can't see how you could do this without getting it on your clothing or yourself in some way. It may be very fine drops, but I would expect somebody to be blood stained.

Did anyone spot someone fleeing the area near Robinson's Field the day Judith was murdered? Police would need to examine the dozens of statements taken from Judith's neighbours and other Tamworth residents regarding the day she went missing.

Chapter Four

Viewed in the Most Serious Light

With today's standards of policing so high and with a number of high-tech tests available that can match the name of a perpetrator to a cluster of cells taken from crime scene evidence, it is easy to forget that historical cases cannot be held to the same standards as today. The investigation into Judith's killer came at a time before police had computers and DNA profiling was still fourteen years away from being developed. The most up to date forensic analysis at the time was the ability to lift fingerprints from clothing, a technique that had only been developed that decade. The process, known as forensic vacuum metal deposition, involved coating an item with atomic layers of metal in a vacuum chamber to reveal a print and was the work of the Home Office, Police Scientific Development Branch.

Police declared that all males in the area would be asked to submit their fingerprints to rule them out of the enquiry. As many as 200 detectives collected more than 15,400 sets of fingerprints and more than 11,000 statements. In addition, officers visited over 11,000 addresses as they made house to house enquiries. Roadblocks were established in the area and 4,200 separate pieces of evidence were followed up.

Originally the incident room had been set up at Tamworth Police Station but was moved to St Editha's Church Hall on College Lane in Wigginton in August 1972, under the leadership of DCS Wright, who became the SIO in the case. New Scotland Yard were brought into the enquiry with their murder squad expertise, under the leadership of DCS Saunders.

***

The work of a major incident room cannot be easily equated with routine police work, although there is a common element so far as it involves the receipt and recording of information from members of the public. Much of the work involves creating and searching indexes. Most of this work is outside the experience of most officers. The hub of a major enquiry is the incident room where all written information is gathered from members of the public, enquiry officers and other sources. The information is channelled using a set of administrative procedures into a system used by the SIO to direct and control the course of the inquiry. The standard procedures are designed to be easy to implement and to be effective in major investigations.

The principal objectives of an incident room controlling a major investigation are:

1. To provide the SIO with an accurate record of all relevant information relating to the crime, together with the police enquiries made and results obtained from there.
2. To show the state of the enquiry and how much work in the form of outstanding actions remains to be done at any one time.
3. To provide all officers with a means of acquiring all previous knowledge of any person, vehicle, address or subject coming into the system which is pertinent to their enquiries.
4. To keep records in a manner that highlights people, vehicles or other factors which have become subject to enquiry in order that such records are capable of pinpointing suspects to whom the SIO may direct special attention.

5. To act as a means of historical reference so that in a long running protracted enquiry, officers joining the investigation team can have easy reference to major police policy decisions taken at earlier stages of the enquiry.
6. To facilitate at the conclusion of the investigation the production of a comprehensive report for legal consideration.
7. To ensure that all information is recorded and linked with the standardised procedural rules of the system so that it may be readily retrieved to aid the SIO and their enquiry teams to establish priorities and to ensure the best possible use is made of staff and equipment in order that all enquiries are made speedily and effectively and the results properly analysed.

All information received was recorded on one of the following forms:

1. Messages
2. Actions
3. Statements
4. Teleprinter messages
5. Officers' reports
6. PDFs
7. Questionnaires
8. Other documents
9. Standard indexes maintained
10. Nominal index
11. Street index
12. Telephone index
13. Vehicle index
14. Category index
15. Sequence of events index

The functions within an incident room are to provide for the flow of information and the posts are:

Senior Investigating Officer
Has the responsibility for the investigation of the crime, liaison with other senior officers, the setting up of an incident room with appropriate accommodation, equipment and manpower. Regular assessment must be made of the work outstanding to ensure a correct staff level to facilitate the process of documents in the most efficient manner.

Deputy to the SIO
Has the responsibility for the control and direction of the investigation in the absence of the SIO.

Office Manager
Has the delegated responsibility for the efficient running of an incident room, maintaining a staffing level capable of carrying out the administrative duties required in the most efficient manner and ensuring that all relevant information is made available to the SIO to assist them in directing the enquiry. They must, at all times, be aware of developments in the investigation and ensure that the SIO is kept abreast of such developments. They must ensure that all staff carry out their specific functions and read all relevant documentation, ensure that all actions raised are dealt with satisfactorily.

Administration Officer
Coordinates all administration with regard to staff, vehicles, accommodation, refreshments, equipment, expenses claims, payment, duty rosters and welfare and to relieve the SIO and OM of all administration matters not connected with the investigation itself.

Receiver
Reads all documents entering the incident room, checks actions correctly completed and endorse results. They assess whether the need for any further action to be raised from the returned action or an urgent action to be raised from the accompanying documents. Then forward all documents to the indexer/action writer. The receiver will be the officer with the most up to date overall picture in respect to the current state of the enquiry and must ensure that all significant developments are brought to the immediate attention of the OM in order that the SIO may be informed.

Action Allocator
Allocates individual actions to members of the enquiry team in accordance with the policy of the SIO and assesses the order of priority for the allocation of these and ensures that each action is allocated to the officer (or officers) able to perform the task required. Provide briefings where necessary to members of the enquiry team ensuring the researcher supplies appropriate documentation so that the ET are fully conversant with their duties in respect of individual actions. Also maintain a detailed record of the state of the incomplete actions.

Statement Reader
They read in detail all statements and reports after they have been typed and all other documents, indicating where actions are to be raised for further enquiries and underlines any content including sequence of events to be indexed and attaches a summary of the statement in the top left-hand corner of the statement. Three copies of the marked-up document are then forwarded to the SIO, OM and indexer/action writer.

Indexer/Researcher/Action Writer
A team of two people working together, who receive all documents from the receiver or statement reader and raises any necessary actions

as instructed after first checking the index to ensure that the enquiry required is not already the subject of a previous action thus avoiding duplication of work. The other person, with access to the index then indexes the content of the documents following the guide established by the statement reader or receiver and includes any other relevant information, making sure that the documents are cross referenced and updated from information held within the index. The indexer must also act as researcher and interrogate the system as it is updated to link the relevant facts and take appropriate action and not merely record the information.

Telephonist
Receives and records all telephone and verbal messages concerning the enquiry and allocates a consecutive number and forwards the messages to the receiver.

Clerk
The Clerk performs all duties in the incident room in connection with photocopying filing and updating documents. Working in conjunction with the incident room but not necessarily within it, will be an exhibits officer and house to house enquiries officer. Procedures for generating enquiries. An action for a specific enquiry will be raised from within the incident room and allocated to an enquiry officer, on completion of that enquiry the result will be returned to the incident room by endorsing the action with the result. This may be accompanied by a statement, an officer's report or a PDF. The returned information will be evaluated and where necessary further actions raised for enquiries to be made and the contents of the returned documents will be indexed into the system to enable the information therein to be retrieved.

***

Of the many pieces of evidence in Judith's case, the recollections of witnesses who had seen her in her final hours alive were paramount in helping police establish her route and to determine when she had been killed and who might have been in and around Robinson's Field at the time of her murder. Ann Dailly of 19 Mildenhall Road, which was on the junction with Lakenheath Road, was looking out of her living room window at around 6.00 pm, which faces onto the forecourt and, at that time, overlooked the butcher's and greengrocer's shops halfway down Lakenheath, which closed at 5.30 pm. She saw a young girl who fitted the description of Judith wearing a dark blue anorak and riding a bicycle along Lakenheath towards her address. Today the butcher's shop and greengrocers are long gone, replaced by a grocer's chain and hair salon adjacent to a children's play area but the view down Lakenheath remains largely unobscured. According to Ann Dailly, the girl she spotted as she looked out of her lounge window stopped at the shops and wheeled across to them, before almost immediately getting back on her bicycle and turning around and cycling back the same way she had come towards Borough Road. As she was doing this Ann Dailly saw a grey-coloured saloon car go onto the forecourt and turn around and go in the same direction as the girl on the bicycle. This was a very important sighting when you consider events that unfolded later concerning a grey car and was not picked up on at the time.

Melvin Roger Hunt of 15 Mildenhall was in his front garden between 6.20 and 6.30 pm tending his roses when he claimed that he saw Judith cycle past from the direction of Brown's Lane turning left into Lakenheath towards Borough Road.

A 14-year-old school boy, Stephen Philip Robinson, at about 6.25 pm on 7 June 1972, walked via Mildenhall Road from his home in Brown's Lane to his friend's address situated in Comberford Road. As he arrived at the junction of Wellsbourne, with Mildenhall near the junction with Chestnut Avenue and Wigginton Road, he saw Judith, the time exactly 6.30 pm as he checked his watch, riding slowly out of Mildenhall and turning right out of Wigginton Road towards Wigginton Village. So, this places Judith's sighting and the grey-coloured car seen by Ann Dailly about 6.25 pm and not 6.00 pm.

At about 6.20 pm, Anthony John Sheldon was driving on the Harlaston to Tamworth Road situated to the north of Wigginton, travelling into Wigginton itself. He passed over the railway bridge and just after passing Wigginton Fields Farm on his nearside, continued through the S-bends into Wigginton Village. He became aware of a highly polished fairly new Ford Escort saloon travelling behind him, which looked maroon in the intensely bright evening sunlight.

Just after passing the junction with Comberford Lane on his offside and approaching the junction with Syerscote Lane on his nearside, where there were some white coloured cottages, he became aware of a young girl on a green-coloured bicycle pedalling towards him and the junction with Comberford Lane, who he described as being in her mid-teens and similar in description to that of Judith, wearing a dark-coloured anorak. By this time, the Ford Escort was close behind and Sheldon in his interior mirror saw the driver glance to his right as he passed the girl. The Escort braked hard and reversed into a gateway before heading off in the direction the girl had ridden off. Anthony Sheldon only had a very vague impression of the driver.

Shirley Simmons of 134 Main Road, Wigginton, was looking out of the window of her living room, which gave a view of the Wigginton end of Comberford Lane, when she saw a girl dressed like Judith with a blue and white dress and a blue covered over garment cycling very slowly down Comberford Lane away from Wigginton around about 6.40 to 6.45 pm.

Another witness, Barry Alsop of 3 Main Road, Wigginton, on 14 June 1972, said:

I am employed by Wigginton Manor Farm as a farm labourer. Last Wednesday evening, the 7th of June 1972 I was in my bedroom at home getting changed. It was between 6:55 pm and 7:00 pm. My bedroom looks across the fields towards Comberford Village and I can see Comberford Lane. I glanced out of my window and saw a grey blue Ford Escort saloon car, backed into the gateway of the field where I am working now. It was about 10 yards inside the gateway. If it hadn't been backed in and side on to me, I wouldn't have known what sort of vehicle it was. I couldn't see anybody in it.

To us this is the most significant sighting of a motor vehicle placed at the murder scene at precisely the time that the pathologist concluded that Judith was killed. The incident room should have been concentrating its efforts on other sightings of this car.

It also ties in with other witness statements taken, firstly that of Ann Dailly. At 6.00 pm she saw a young girl who fitted the description of Judith wearing a dark blue anorak riding a bicycle along Lakenheath towards her address. The girl stopped at the shops and wheeled across to them and almost immediately got back on her bicycle, turned around and cycled back the way she had come towards Borough Road. As she was doing this, Ann Dailly saw a grey-coloured saloon car go onto the forecourt and turn around and go in the same direction as the girl on the bicycle. This was a very important sighting not picked up on when you consider events that unfolded later concerning a grey car. If the witness had been shown a chart of cars, she could easily have narrowed them down to a make and model.

Police enquiries revealed that on the evening of Judith's murder, Comberford Lane had been a hive of activity and a number of witnesses were traced. As a result, seven different vehicles seen using the lane during the material time were sought for tracing, implication or elimination.

The *Tamworth Herald* ran a series of articles on the case, including a report on Friday, 23 June 1972: ITN footage shows a flurry of activity in the fields where Judith's body was found. Verges and ditches are inspected by search officers clearly looking for a murder weapon and other clues discarded by Judith's attacker. It was reported in the *Tamworth Herald* a week later that the murder weapon had been found but police would not say what it was, a fingerprint was found on Judith's bicycle and as a result a massive fingerprint operation of the local male population was undertaken.

This was featured in the *Tamworth Herald* on Friday, 30 June 1972 at that time the police were focussing their attention on tracing a dirty-blue Ford Cortina car, 1963 or 1964 model, seen near the murder spot, and also a red or maroon car and a white Triumph 2000. So, clearly the lane was busy with passing and parked traffic during the evening of 7 June 1972:

> Detective Chief Superintendent Wright said a number of people who use the lane 'at the material time had been traced and had provided a lot of useful information.'

The *Tamworth Herald* ran a series of articles on the case, including this report on Friday, 23 June 1972:

> THIRTEEN days have gone by since the battered body of 14-year-old Judith Roberts was found lying beside her green bicycle in a field off Comberford Lane of the outskirts of Tamworth ... Since then, between 80 and 100 detectives have been working day and night in the hunt for a brutal killer.

At the beginning of September 1972, they issued three photo kit pictures of three men seen in or around Comberford Lane during the evening of 7 June 1972; none remotely fitted the later rent-a-suspect.

While police hunted for a 'sexually depraved killer', the local community were still rocked by Judith's murder. Her family laid her to rest at St Editha's parish church, in Tamworth, where Judith had worshipped, on 24 June 1972. The day was somewhat of a juxtaposition for the town, with Judith's funeral procession taking part in the morning before the annual carnival commenced in the afternoon. Sombre bells rang in the morning, while funfair music blared from the grounds of Tamworth Castle in the afternoon. Part of Judith's last journey to her place of rest would include driving past part of the route she took on her last cycle. On the young victim's coffin, a single wreath of pink and white carnations in the shape of a cross rested. A posy with the signatures of all her classmates further was among one of eighty-six flower tributes expressing love and sorrow to the young girl. As well as her family and friends, Queen Elizabeth Grammar School headmaster Bernard Baker, DCS Saunders, DCS Wright, and Lichfield Police Division Chief Superintendent Ben Taylor paid their respects to Judith. The school's music master, Graham Parsons, played the organ. Hundreds of people lined the pavements outside the church as the service took place. Reverend Albert Edwards said:

> Judith was an extremely nice girl. Her tragic death has come as a terrible shock to all who knew her.

Chapter Five

Connecting the Dots

Ask yourself, of all the many vehicles you see on your morning commute, or of all the lorries you pass on the motorway – outside of maybe a sparse company logo, could you describe one distinguishable feature about any of them? It is at this stage we would like to introduce the crimes of a killer whose *modus operandi* heavily mirrors those of Judith's brutal murder. Their crimes were still several years from being brought to the public's attention but when thrust into the centre of a police investigation were so voluminous that they threatened to collapse the very building that housed them. The crimes of Peter William Sutcliffe.

Sutcliffe was born in Bingley in summer 1946 to parents John William Sutcliffe and Kathleen Frances. The boy was raised, as were his five siblings, Roman Catholic – something of an homage to his mother's Catholic roots in Ireland. Sutcliffe left school at the age of 15 and started a series of menial jobs, including two stints as a gravedigger in the 1960s. Sutcliffe was a loner as a child; social skills were not his strong suit. Between November 1971 and April 1973, he found employment with the Baird Television factory in Bradford, approximately 110 miles south along the (at this time, still relatively new) M1 motorway, working on a packaging line. By the time of Judith's murder in 1972, Sutcliffe was an unknown entity to many police forces. The 26-year-old's rap sheet would show he had received a fine for 'going equipped to steal' and a caution for an assault against a sex worker in Bradford. The truth of these offences was much more sinister.

Sutcliffe, had a driving licence and also a growing propensity for violence which would culminate into convictions for thirteen grotesque murders as well as attempts on the lives of seven other women – all this under the ultimate disguise: the innocuous tradesman's lorry. Sutcliffe used this indistinguishable transit to his advantage. Prior to his incarceration, the hunt for the man roaming the north of England with a hammer and sharpened screwdriver would send police on a six-year frenzied manhunt. It was then, and remains today, the largest and most expensive manhunt in British history.

The state of Judith's partially hidden body is glaringly similar to the state of multiple victims of Sutcliffe – their injuries inflicted with a hammer and sharpened screwdriver heavily resemble those of Judith's and our belief is that a heavy/walling hammer was used in her murder. With that in mind, we turned our attention to Sutcliffe's MO. Could he really have committed Judith's murder?

In 2020, when researching this book, a former Staffordshire police officer (known only as 'Officer A') spoke with us in relation to the connection between Judith and Sutcliffe. His belief was that Sutcliffe could not have been the killer, his theory propped up by the following points:

1. Judith had the appearance of a child, not an adult (giving way to the theory that Sutcliffe only attacked adults).
2. The murder occurred during the daylight (suggesting that Sutcliffe did only attack under the cover of complete darkness).
3. The locus is out in the countryside along a narrow lane, which might just accommodate a tractor (highlighting the difficult road conditions surrounding the area where Judith was found).
4. The nearest trunk road is some 5/6 miles away (further highlighting the above).

The Murder of Judith Roberts

While certainly interesting points to raise, it forced us to look more closely at the circumstances around Sutcliffe's known attacks. If we were to suggest that Sutcliffe was responsible then we would need to take a hard look at his MO, his offending history and his prevalences for attacking.

The story of how Sutcliffe came to be one of the worst serial killers in British criminal history is one that has been told and retold for decades – in fact, his story has often overshadowed that of the scores of women he was convicted of attacking and killing. As a result, the general public do not remember these women for their abilities to light up a room with their laughter, nor are they remembered by the masses as great mothers to their children, or the gentle caring friend who was a shoulder to cry on, their identities instead condensed into a monochromic face in a grid and a name on a list that is displayed in the press wherever Sutcliffe is mentioned – their names:

Wilma McCann, aged 28
Emily Jackson, aged 42
Irene Richardson, aged 28
Patricia 'Tina' Atkinson, aged 32
Jayne MacDonald, aged 16
Jean Jordan, aged 20
Yvonne Pearson, aged 21
Helen Rytka, aged 18
Vera Millward, aged 40
Josephine Whitaker, aged 19
Barbara Leach, aged 20
Marguerite Walls, aged 47
Jacqueline Hill, aged 20

Thanks largely to the press, their autonomy as women ceased to exist the day their names were printed next to the word 'victim'. There are a great deal of books that have been written, as well as research compiled, which have sought rightly so to reprieve these women, if only for a few short pages, from this role, of being merely a 'prostitute', 'good time girl' or 'victim of Peter Sutcliffe' and written instead about their lives as individuals. These women were far more than the occupations listed next to their names and were worth far more than the fate they suffered.

Sutcliffe's criminal history dates as far back as 1963. This was for what were considered 'misdemeanour offences' then but, in hindsight, were the beginning of a 17-year escalation of crimes. In 1963 and 1964, Sutcliffe, aged 17 and 18 at the time, had his first run-ins with the law for motor offences. He was stopped and reported by Keighley Police for driving a car unaccompanied and failing to display L-Plates. On a Sunday night in March 1965, when he was aged 19, Sutcliffe was seen with another person trying the door handles of several unattended motor vehicles in Old Main Street, Bingley, beside the River Aire. Both were arrested for attempting to steal from an unattended motor vehicle and appeared at Bingley West Riding Magistrates Court on 17 May 1965. For this offence, Sutcliffe was fined 5 pounds; ironically the same amount of money that would almost lead to his capture thirteen years later when a 5 pound note paid by Sutcliffe would be discovered on a woman he had murdered. In 1965 and 1966 Sutcliffe would gain yet more motor convictions. These 'victimless' crimes aside, Sutcliffe's first known attack was carried out in August 1969 against an unnamed woman whom he smacked over the head with a piece of brick in a sock. Sutcliffe, then a 23-year-old cemetery worker, had been going steady with his girlfriend (and future wife), Sonia Szurma, for two years at this time. The plan was that the pair would marry once she was a qualified teacher. Those plans seemed to be on the rocks though after Sutcliffe's brother Mick spotted her in a sports car with an Italian man, a local ice cream salesman. *Somebody's Husband,*

Somebody's Son: The Story of the Yorkshire Ripper by Gordon Burn explicitly details how the events unfolded and how Sutcliffe's first known attack on a woman transpired. When confronted by Sutcliffe, Sonia admitted she had been in the company of this gentleman, and the competition for Sutcliffe was too much to bear. Weeks after he found out about the Italian man in the sports car, he approached a sex worker at a petrol station along Manningham Lane in Bradford in the hope of 'getting even' with his partner for what he evidently felt was a betrayal. However, he couldn't go through with it, later recalling how the woman, who he deemed to be 'coarse and vulgar', had repulsed him. However, the sex worker in question allegedly scammed Sutcliffe out of £10, forcing him to leave the situation empty handed and further humiliated. He no doubt felt enraged that, once again, a woman had made a fool of him. What's more, Sutcliffe realised that Sonia was seeing this 'Italian Stallion' multiple times a week. As Gordon Burns writes in his biography:

> Inevitably, they [Sutcliffe and Sonia] spent the whole time arguing, which is all they seemed to do whenever they saw each other for a long time.

Approximately three weeks later, Sutcliffe approached the sex worker, who he claimed had conned him, in a public house in Lumb Lane and gave her the opportunity to right the wrong he felt he had been done. She laughed in his face and encouraged those within earshot to join in the joke that was Sutcliffe. No more than a month after the incident, when out drinking with his friend, Trevor Birdsall, something evidently snapped inside Sutcliffe. It was a Saturday evening in early September 1969 that Sutcliffe's criminal record began, in what became known as the 'stone in the sock' incident. Had it been documented properly at the time; it would have been a strong indicator for Sutcliffe's future attacks and could have possibly stopped the escalation of murders and attempted murders. Sutcliffe, was riding as a passenger in Birdsall's car as the pair drove along St Paul's Road in Manningham Park. Sutcliffe suddenly exited the vehicle. He had set his sights on a completely random bypasser, a woman who he himself had identified was a sex worker. Sutcliffe claimed that he followed her to a house somewhere and had hit her on the back of her head with a 'stone' in a sock. After hopping back in the vehicle 'fairly quickly', Birdsall would later tell Sir Michael Havers in court that Sutcliffe 'looked a bit excited and was not breathing normally' as though he had possibly been running. When asked by Havers if Sutcliffe had said anything upon entering the vehicle, Birdsall replied:

> He just told me to drive off. I asked him where he had been, and he said he had followed a woman to a house somewhere. He said he had hit her, I'm not too sure. He mentioned something about some money, but I can't remember too well.

Despite a swift whack to the head, the woman had the quick wit to make a note of Birdsall's registration number and the next day two police officers visited Sutcliffe at his home at 57 Cornwall Road, in Bingley. Sutcliffe admitted hitting the woman but claimed it was only with his hand. He was given a stern lecture and cautioned by the officers. The victim, for her own reasons, did not press charges against Sutcliffe. Forgetting the absence of a case file, this was grade one intelligence on Sutcliffe being capable of aggravated assault and it should have been indexed in the collator system and passed to force and region intelligence for future use.

At Sutcliffe's murder trial during 1981, his defence barrister James Armstrong Chadwin asked Sutcliffe why he had attacked the woman in September 1969, whose case is outlined above, and Sutcliffe replied: 'I was attempting to kill her' and he further went on to say that:

> I got out of the car, went across the road and hit her. The force of the impact tore the toe off the sock and whatever was in it came out. I went back to the car and got in it.

This first known attack sets the precedent for the next eleven years of Sutcliffe's life and serves as a blueprint for what would be a series of grotesque and demonstrable attacks and murders. In the book, *Voices from an Evil God: The True Story of the Yorkshire Ripper and the Woman Who Loved Him* by Barbara Jones (Blake Publishing, 1991), Sutcliffe claimed that this attack happened in the afternoon. By contrast, Gordon Burns's book, *Somebody's Husband, Somebody's Son: The Story of the Yorkshire Ripper*, and trial testimony suggest it happened at night. If Jones' book is correct, it would show that in his infancy as a killer; Sutcliffe was not honed enough in his homicidal habits to operate under the darkness of night, which could have been the case for some years considering he got off with only a warning for his attack. Could he have still been operating under such circumstances three years later when Judith was killed? At the very least it would indicate that Sutcliffe did not always operate within the shadows of darkness.

Within weeks of the police cautioning Sutcliffe about the 'stone in the sock' incident, which was recorded as an aggravated assault, Sutcliffe was to be arrested again. On Monday, 29 September 1969, Sutcliffe was in the Manningham area. Sutcliffe again went out looking for vulnerable women to attack. This time he took a hammer and a long-bladed knife into the Manningham area. He recalled at his trial in 1981:

> I were [sic] driving me [my] old Morris Minor and I were [sic] looking for a prostitute. I knew this were [sic] the mission I had to carry out. The voices told me it wasn't good enough just to attack them. I had to do it properly. I had to kill.

Sutcliffe was observed by the police sitting in his vehicle, deliberately trying to look unobtrusive, with the engine running quietly and the lights off. When a police officer called PC Bland approached the car, Sutcliffe drove off at high speed. A search of the area was carried out and the policeman again spotted Sutcliffe's car a short distance away, this time parked and unattended with the lights on and the engine running. On closer inspection the officer discovered Sutcliffe hunched behind a privet hedge within a private garden with a hammer in his hand. Sutcliffe told the officer that a hubcap had flown off his front wheel and that he had been looking for it and the hammer was to help him secure it in place.

Suspecting that Sutcliffe's story was fabricated and suspicious, he nicked him for being in possession of an offensive weapon, suggesting that Sutcliffe had been equipped for a burglary/theft. Under the circumstances that Sutcliffe had been found in, most 'streetwise coppers' today would have nicked him for being in possession of an offensive weapon and searched him at the scene before he got into the police van as a matter of routine. Searching a suspect at the scene would be a routine task that had been instilled at training school. This is done for two reasons: firstly, to obtain evidence of a crime, and secondly, to prevent injury to the officer or offender. This search would have revealed the presence of the knife that Sutcliffe later claimed he had slipped down a gap between the side of the police vehicle and the wheel arch cover inside the police van that came to collect him. Astonishingly, Sutcliffe wasn't searched at the scene. Twelve years later Sutcliffe would again hide weapons when arrested in 1981.

During this earlier occasion, having been stopped in September 1969, Sutcliffe went into Bradford Police Station. Sir Lawrence Byford's report, written by the chief inspector of constabulary in 1981 about West Yorkshire Police's failings in the Sutcliffe investigation, which was published by the Home Office in 2006, making reference to the lull between this and his first known murder in 1975 says: 'He

(Sutcliffe) was not suspected by the police of having the hammer for the purpose of inflicting violence to the person and the meagre police records remaining show that he was subsequently charged with "going equipped for stealing.'" Sutcliffe was photographed and fingerprinted and appeared at the magistrates' court two weeks later in October 1969 and was fined £25.

There were many failings and missed opportunities in the investigation into Sutcliffe, but one of the gravest of all is the recording of Sutcliffe's earliest crime. It was an error and/or oversight that could have saved many lives. As was routine, a local and national check would have been made to see if there was anything known about him and that should have thrown up the local caution a couple of weeks earlier, but the records had been weeded out alongside other inactive offences such as shoplifting and road traffic offences. Here a huge opportunity was missed to link him to the caution for the 'stone in the sock' assault and this offence. Coupled with the fact that both offences were committed in notoriously known areas and that the first involved a sex worker, Sutcliffe would have then been viewed, correctly, as a danger to women and recorded as such at force headquarters and in New Scotland Yard's method index. Although it was an arrest for a minor offence, it was a very unusual potential method of attack, so a copy of the crime form went straight to New Scotland Yard to be placed in their index – the New Scotland Yard method index – which was available to all police forces. The method index was well established as a tool for all police forces to use in identifying suspects who had committed similar crimes using the same method. After this, his name could come up as a possible suspect for any offences in the country where a hammer was used – if anybody checked the index – but the horror is that nobody did. There were twelve regional crime intelligence officers with a desk each within C11 (later SO11), composed of officers from a number of integrated intelligence-led forces set up to deal with cross border and cross region travelling criminals, for example, the North West Region consisted of Cheshire Constabulary, Derbyshire Constabulary and Staffordshire Police.

Sutcliffe's details, following his arrest in 1969, were placed in a central method index. The file collated all the methods of attack used by criminals to help police forces across the country to link crimes. Senior Metropolitan Police detectives did assist other police forces in the country on serious cases, as they did in the case of Judith, and should have searched the method index for anyone who had used a hammer on a victim. That file could have identified the serial killer in the making years before he went on to brutally murder many other women before his final capture in 1981. If this index had been checked at any point during the six-year investigation to uncover his identity, it might have prevented the deaths of more than a dozen. Similarly, such a search would have then catapulted him to the top of any suspects list later in 1975 when Anna Rogulskyj was attacked, and would have saved a lot of women's lives, as well as countless enquiries, mountains of paperwork and files, and ridicule from the public.

Sutcliffe's conviction for this first offence was recorded both at West Riding CRO and Bradford City Police Collator but with no reference to a hammer. Whereas New Scotland Yard, who had the same copy of the conviction recorded it 'Equipped for stealing (hammer)' and under 'method' the words 'In possession of housebreaking implement by night namely a hammer'.

There are no confirmed attacks by Sutcliffe after the 1969 incident for almost six years. The Byford report would also notice this quiet period for Sutcliffe, stating:

> There is a curious and unexplained lull in Sutcliffe's criminal activities.

The report continues:

> It is my firm conclusion that between 1969 and 1980 Sutcliffe was probably responsible for many attacks on unaccompanied women, which he has not yet admitted, not only in the West Yorkshire and Manchester areas but also in other parts of the country.

The Byford Report, in its entirety, has not been disclosed to the public. 'Description of suspects, photofits and other assaults' and other parts of the section on Sutcliffe's 'immediate associates' remain under lock and key. It is not clear when or if they shall ever be released. A curious detail in the chronology is that of twenty-two confirmed murders, the longest Sutcliffe staved off his murderous impulses was 353 days, less than one year, between the attacks on Barbara Leach in September 1979 and Marguerite Walls in August 1980.

The woman often referred to as Sutcliffe's 'first victim' is Anna Rogulskyj. Known as 'Irish Annie', she lived in Keighley, West Yorkshire, and worked in Woolworths. A 36-year-old woman, Carol Ann Lee describes her in her book, *Somebody's Mother, Somebody's Daughter: True Stories from Victims and Survivors of the Yorkshire Ripper* (Michael O'Mara Books, 2019), as someone who was going through what would today be identified as a toxic and tumultuous relationship with her partner, Geoffrey Hughes. Come the day of her attack, 5 July 1975, five years and ten months after what would become known as the 'stone in the sock' incident, Anna had had her fill of frustration. As well as her volatile relationship with Hughes, she had been pestered recently by a particularly persistent man, who she had come face to face with twice already in recent weeks. This man, who she would later recall as having 'racing' eyes, 'dainty' hands and a mass of thick dark hair on his head and face, and who police would later identify as Sutcliffe, had first approached her in the street in summer 1975 and asked her to join him for a cup of tea. She had declined and managed to shake him from her step. However, the same man made a second advance a few weeks later only to receive a similar, if not slightly more aggressive rejection. But on Friday, 4 July 1975 she and Hughes had a particularly bad quarrel. She had stormed over to his home in North Queen Street in the early hours of Saturday morning. On her way, the man with the 'dainty' hands and 'racing' eyes (Sutcliffe) appeared again, like a bad smell Anna was unable to shake off. Undeterred by her earlier rejections, he propositioned her, asking her if she 'fancied it'.

'Not on your life' Anna shot back. She was a woman on a mission and not at all interested in a random stranger. When she reached Hughes' home in North Queen Street she banged on the door and window, but he did not answer. Anna could have waited on his doorstep but perhaps she had decided enough was enough and that returning home seemed like the more viable option now that it was growing late. Anna decided to turn back; the distance between her own home and Hughes's was only ten minutes. Barely a few streets away, the small man with 'dainty' hands and a thick Yorkshire accent made another appearance and asked her to have sex with him. Anna's answer was followed with a swift jab to his ribs with her elbow but this time he was undeterred and he hit back from behind, smashing Anna over the head with a hammer. She survived, but unfortunately her attacker wasn't picked up by police. Carol Ann Lee draws a heartbreaking picture in her book as she describes how friends and family of Anna recalled how the attack had clear psychological effects on her and the once fiery and vivacious woman was forever changed. What can we draw from Sutcliffe's attack on Anna? We can see that he acted alone and approached his victims and engaged in conversation with them. He clearly had no issue approaching his victims in broad daylight, as we can see from his tactless and tasteless attempts to entice Anna in the weeks leading up to her attack, trying to encourage her to spend time with him. The attack itself took place at night – Anna was found by a passerby at 2.20 am and rushed to Leeds General Infirmary where surgeons saved her life.

Sutcliffe's second attack took place the following month, only forty days after he attacked Anna, on Friday, 15 August 1975. Sutcliffe spotted 46-year-old office cleaner Olive Smelt, who was having a drink with friends at a pub called The Royal Oak in Halifax, West Yorkshire. Sutcliffe was there drinking with his friend at the time, Trevor Birstall, and made a snide remark within earshot of the mother of three about her being a 'prostitute'. Olive set him straight and publicly rebuked his remarks. Whether it was the public humiliation or his stern belief that Olive was a sex worker, Sutcliffe made the decision to punish Olive. As the pubs were turning out at closing time, he spotted her as she walked home after accepting a lift from friends to Boothtown Road, just moments from her home. Spotting her in the dark and alone, he approached Olive. 'The weather's let us down a bit, hasn't it?' he sang in his Yorkshire accent before he hit her across the head with a hammer. Olive's neighbour was returning home and his headlights blared into the face of Sutcliffe while he attacked Olive. He then made off, disturbed and unable to finish his attack to its full capacity. Like his previous target, Olive survived. Olive later mentioned to police that her attacker spoke with a Yorkshire accent. Police linked Anna's and Olive's attacks to the same perpetrator.

The next attack carried out by Sutcliffe was on Wednesday, 27 August 1975. This time the lone female would not be a woman in her thirties or forties, but on a child: 14-year-old Tracy Browne in Silsden, West Yorkshire. Tracy has bravely recounted her story multiple times over the years, including as part of the Network First documentary *Silent Victims: The Untold Story of The Yorkshire Ripper* in 1996. Produced in the wake of The Byford Report, it was one of the first documentaries to publicly declare that the true tally of Sutcliffe's victims was beyond the scope of what he had been charged with. The day she was attacked, Tracy had been out with her friends and twin sister Mandy for the day and had decided to walk home to the quiet farm where she lived with Mandy, her mother Nora and father Tony.

The walk home would take about thirty minutes and at around 10.15 pm she decided to begin her journey. Tracy's sister had already walked ahead, while Tracy talked to her friends. When she walked home, she was alone, until she reached the lane on approach to her home. Almost out of nowhere, a man with dark eyes and hair appeared ahead of her. His eyes found Tracy if only for a moment but he carried on walking, only to slow down and engage in a conversation with the young girl further up the road. He introduced himself as Tony Jennis. The pair engaged in small talk for roughly thirty minutes as they walked towards Tracy's home. She often recalls how, despite how glaringly obvious it is now that this was a heinous individual, she never once felt in danger from this man. On two occasions 'Jennis' stopped, once to blow his nose and once to tie his shoelace, each time falling behind her but eventually catching up to her again. As Tracy reached her home, she went to bid him goodbye and thank him for the pleasant conversation when the man lunged at her, striking her over the head five times with a ball pein hammer. Luckily, the rumbling wheels of a passing motorist disturbed this attack and Sutcliffe threw his stunned victim over a barbed wire fence before making off. Tracy managed to stumble home and, like Anna and Olive, survived her attack after being rushed to hospital.

Thanks to her prolonged conversation with the man who attacked her, Tracy later recalled to police that the man was 5 foot 8 inches in height, had dark Afro-type hair and a full beard. He also had a gap between his teeth and spoke in a high-pitched voice with a Yorkshire accent. From memory she was able to produce an uncanny artist's impression of Sutcliffe, which appeared in the *Keighley News*. The sketch was printed on posters that were distributed throughout the locality. For years police didn't believe she had been attacked by the same man they were chasing for the attacks on other women – in their opinion, she was too young and the attack was carried out earlier in the day than many of Sutcliffe's other attacks. Again, Sutcliffe had no problem approaching his target. What if Judith, like Tracy, was making her way home when she was attacked? The medical report could not ascertain the exact time that she was murdered. Due to how long it had been since she had gone missing, they could only suggest she had been killed three days prior.

Tracy's attack is particularly significant because it shows that Sutcliffe did not discriminate in his selection of victim – age, occupation, physical attributes had no meaning in his attacks, despite Sutcliffe's claims to police on his arrest that he was acting out a 'crusade' against sex workers, a command of God he was given from a graveside in Bingley. What's more, Tracy was the exact same age Judith was when she was attacked. Her attack was carried out less than three years after Judith's. Their hometowns are approximately 130 miles apart, at either end of the M1 motorway. A survivor of Sutcliffe at only 14 years old makes it clear he did not only attack grown women. Sutcliffe later admitted he thought Tracy was older than she was. Could the same be true of Judith?

At the time of Tracy's attack, Sutcliffe was a lorry driver and living in Heaton, Newcastle, approximately 100 miles away, so evidently Sutcliffe had no issue with travelling hundreds of miles to carry out his attacks, something we would later see in the attack on Barbara Leach, who was killed during a 400-mile round trip that Sutcliffe drove for work. Tracy's attack would not be connected to Sutcliffe until after his arrest in 1981 and he would not confess to attacking her until 1992, when questioned by West Yorkshire Police's assistant chief constable. It is not unreasonable to assume that had Tracy not recalled her attacker so vividly that Sutcliffe may never have confessed to her attack. In the meantime, he was free to carry on committing horrific crimes against other vulnerable victims. The next woman to fall prey to Sutcliffe's sick and perverse ways, Wilma McCann, unlike Anna, Olive and Tracy, would not survive.

Wilma's murder on Thursday, 30 October 1975 marked a significant period in history. As the first woman to be recognised as an official murder victim of such a serial killer, her story is one that would forever paint a picture of the landscape for not only police and detective work but for sociological attitudes towards those whose lives were one way or another changed by Sutcliffe. Her face is the first image seen on the grid of victims, a photo taken of her by police when she was arrested at 18 years old, along with the damning words that have, for decades, been used in conjunction with her murder: 'well-known prostitute'. Wilma, much like all the other victims, was a daughter, a friend, a woman made up of many nuanced intricacies that only she possessed, and her death was a deeply dark time for those who knew and loved her.

Wilma had struck up a conversation with Sutcliffe on her way home from a night out in Leeds, West Yorkshire, and agreed to have sex with him. Soon after the pair pulled up in his car to the Prince Phillip Playing Field at around 1.30 am, just 100 yards from where she lived, she lay down on the grass and unbuckled her trousers. 'Cummon [come on], get it over with' she urged Sutcliffe. The Yorkshire man had come out this fateful evening equipped and ready to pounce. Sutcliffe struck her over the head with his hammer, raining his weapon down on her skull five times. When he'd finished, he stabbed her nine times in her lower abdomen, inches from where the four children she had brought into the world had once rested safely. She was stabbed twice below her right breast and three times below her left – the breasts she would have used to nurse those children when they were born. She was also stabbed once in the throat, a throat once used to tell her children and friends that she loved them. The site of her body scared the milkman and his 10-year-old younger brother who found her body the next morning. Even veteran police officers who rushed to the scene were disturbed by what they found. Semen was found on the back of her pants and trousers, evidence that her killer had masturbated over her body as she lay dying. A genetic profile obtained from the semen stain showed that the person who had killed Wilma was a non-secretor, meaning that the killer (Sutcliffe) belonged to a group of the population (approximately 20 per cent) who did not secrete blood group antigens into their bodily fluids. The savagery carried out by Sutcliffe on Wilma is something mirrored in numerous attacks at his hand. Judith's body bore a similar amount of mindless, grotesque violence that no one should ever be subjected to. If samples had been taken from that 'glistening trail' on Judith's body, would they have matched the profile found on Wilma's? During 1975, Anna Rogulskyj, Olive Smelt and Tracy Browne were all beaten with a ball pein hammer. But crucially, no check was ever made by police in the New Scotland Yard method index.

Emily Jackson was killed by Sutcliffe on Tuesday, 20 January 1976. Carol Ann Lee's book *Somebody's Mother, Somebody's Daughter: True Stories from Victims and Survivors of the Yorkshire Ripper* describes how Emily, having used sex work as a means to save her family from starvation and her husband's business from collapsing from financial difficulties, had been picked up by Sutcliffe in front of The Gaiety pub in Leeds, West Yorkshire sometime after 7.00 pm. Sutcliffe claims, in his confession to West Yorkshire Police after his arrest in 1981, that it was between 8.00 and 9.00 pm. He drove to Roundhay Road and parked up in a derelict area that was away from the lights of the main road. In this darkened corner he pretended his car wouldn't start. Emily had offered him the light of a lighter she carried with her while he looked under his bonnet to solve the issue. While she held the light in her hand, Sutcliffe took a couple of steps back before pouncing. He struck her over the head twice, with what was noted in her autopsy to be possibly a hammer, before he dragged her body into a nearby yard and killed her. Her sweater, cardigan and bra were pushed up and her pants pulled down before Sutcliffe took out a cross-ply Phillips screwdriver and stabbed her fifty-two times in the heart, front and back, leaving cross shaped impressions on her skin. In an even more degrading act, Sutcliffe thrust a piece of wood between her legs. Sutcliffe was spooked when a car stopped a few yards from where the body of Emily lay. He fled the scene, returning home to his in-laws' house in Clayton, Bradford, less than 20 miles from the murder scene, leaving behind a vital clue that would allude to the identity of the killer: a size 7 Wellington boot print.

Emily's body was found at 8.10 am the following morning. The scene disturbed even the stoic exterior of senior police officer DCS Dennis Hoban who was at the murder site, along with Professor David Gee (the pathologist) and Ron Outteridge (forensics). Her body had been posed, her tights had been pulled down exposing her underwear, and her shoes had been removed; one was near her right foot, while the other had been left near a wall that encased the murder scene. Emily's murder, combined with the attack on Wilma, who had been seen thumbing a lift the night she was killed in the vicinity of Emily's murder scene, as noted by Professor Gee, prompted suspicions that the murders were linked and that the killer was possibly a long-distance lorry driver.

After Emily's attack, the press started to make reference to an infamous historic serial killer, 'Jack the Ripper' – a man who had attacked at least five sex workers in London in 1888. The name, a grim homage, became a damning moniker as it suggested that this killer, like Jack, was also only targeting women who were sex workers. Indeed, this belief began to steer the attitudes within the investigation, bestowing a sociological shame upon these women who fell outside of a stereotypical 'good girl' image. Nonetheless these women were mothers, sisters, aunts and daughters and all worthy of safety and protection. The mere suggestion that only a certain type of person, with a certain type of job or routine or social status, was the only type of person at risk of being victim to this most depraved individual meant that attempts to link victims and survivors to the crimes and ascertain the true picture of Sutcliffe's offending would become increasingly difficult to do, and led to police discounting victims including Anna, Olive and Tracy.

The cross-shaped impressions on Emily's skin are most notable in this case as Judith's pathology report showed a distinct Y-shaped mark on her skull, a shape closely resembling the marks left on Emily's skin. Emily's attack also shows that the time of day was not vitally important, Emily was attacked two or three hours earlier in the evening, although in January, unforgiving daylight would have shielded his identity from the view of any passerby.

Sutcliffe is not identified as having killed anyone until the following year, 1977, but that's not to say he wasn't still on his murderous rampage. Marcella Claxton was attacked on 9 May 1976, in Leeds, West Yorkshire. Marcella, a sex worker, was hit over the head with a hammer eight or nine times by Sutcliffe as she crouched near a tree in Soldiers' Field trying to relieve herself. Sutcliffe, who had picked her up in the early hours of the morning and offered her money for sex, was waiting nearby. She was only saved by a passing car that disturbed Sutcliffe. Marcella's injuries were so significant that she required extensive brain surgery, including fifty-two stitches to the wound on her head. She gave a compelling description of her attacker: a young, white man with crinkly black hair and a beard, he had a Yorkshire accent and had told her he didn't live in Leeds. She even described his white car with its red upholstery. Even with the stark recollection of her attack, hers was not immediately linked to Sutcliffe, despite glaring similarities to Wilma and Emily. Marcella's case was marred with racism; as a woman of colour she sadly wasn't taken seriously by police. Even Sutcliffe himself tried to deny that he had approached Marcella for sex. We firmly believe that had Sutcliffe not been bang to rights over Marcella's attack, and the evidence not so watertight, he would have taken her attack to his grave. Only through her determination and bravery did Marcella manage to see justice done.

Throughout the year of 1977, Sutcliffe is known to have attacked six women:

Irene Richardson, 28 years old, attacked on Saturday, 5 February in Leeds, West Yorkshire.

Patricia Atkinson, 32 years old, attacked on Saturday, 23 April in Bradford, West Yorkshire.

Jayne McDonald, 16 years old, attacked on Sunday, 26 June in Leeds, West Yorkshire.

Maureen Long, 42 years old, attacked on Sunday, 10 July, in Bradford, West Yorkshire.

Jean Jordan, 20 years old, attacked on Saturday, 1 October in Manchester.

Marilyn Moore, 25 years old, attacked on Wednesday, 14 December in Leeds, West Yorkshire.

Only Maureen and Marilyn survived.

Irene was killed in the same spot that Sutcliffe had attacked Marcella, just nine months earlier. Unlike Marcella, Irene would not survive her attack. Interestingly, Sutcliffe changed his weapon of choice when he attacked Irene; having previously favoured a hammer and screwdriver, after three heavy blows to Irene's skull with his hammer, Sutcliffe tore open her jacket and blouse and began to stab and slash at her with his Stanley knife – this shows again that

Sutcliffe's attacks, although largely in keeping with his MO, were changed and altered. Found lying face down with her hands under her body, Irene's legs were covered with her coat. Was this the first time Sutcliffe had concealed his victim? Or had a similar MO been displayed in another unknown victim? One thing we can be certain of, Sutcliffe was an opportunist and preyed on women whenever the mood struck him.

Irene's body had been posed; the boots she had worn the night she was killed were laid along the back of her legs. Her skirt and slip had been hoisted around her waist and her tights removed from her right leg, and her underwear had been tampered with. The watch around her wrist had frozen at 8.50 (pm). The brutality of her injuries reflects those of Sutcliffe's previous murder victims: Irene's throat had been slit and her stomach slashed in three places – all were downward strokes that had resulted in grisly wounds. A semen stain on Irene's tights proved that her killer was, again as was seen in Wilma's murder, a non-secretor.

Unlike the other women who were all attacked and killed in an open space, the next woman Sutcliffe is known to have killed, Patricia, was murdered inside her home at Oak Lane in Bradford – another change to Sutcliffe's favoured methods. Hit on the back of the head four times, Sutcliffe hit Patricia a fifth time before he began to tamper with her body, pulling down her jeans and pants and exposing her breasts. His attack worsened as he hit her repeatedly with the blunt end of his hammer and clawed at her with the other end. The pathology report also showed that there was evidence that her killer had attempted to stab her in the back. She had slash marks along the left side of her body. This attack, also combined with the location that he carried it out is furthermore evidence that Sutcliffe was an opportunist but also that he would amend his MO to suit his surroundings and his own desires. Like Irene, Patricia's body was covered as he left the scene, this time with bed sheets. A size 7 Wellington boot print was found inside her home, similar to the one found at the scene of Emily Jackson's murder.

Jayne McDonald was another child victim of Sutcliffe's. At only 16 years old she was, for a time, considered the youngest victim of the serial killer prowling the north of England. At the time of her murder, she had recently left school. Her attack, the fifth murder and sixth known attack, opened the eyes of the public to the notion that the serial killer on the loose was killing young girls and women, that his victims were not just 'good time girls' or sex workers but that his agenda was something far beyond what they had been led to believe. Again, it is worth pointing out that Sutcliffe murdered a child. She might have left school but Jayne was green to the world.

What we can learn from the murder of Jean Jordan on 1 October 1977, is that Peter Sutcliffe was not confined to the boundaries of West Yorkshire, an important factor to consider when looking at unsolved cases like Judith's that could be connected to him. Sutcliffe regularly travelled down to the likes of London and to Cambridgeshire, where his sister-in-law was living in London. His job, with T&S Clark, gave him access to a vehicle that travelled the country under the guise of a respectable job. Jean, a married sex worker who was trying hard to build a good life for herself and her children was hit over the head eleven times with Sutcliffe's hammer. Professor Gee would need to remould her skull with modelling clay; it was so badly shattered from the impact. Her body was found nine days after she was last seen, in an allotment adjacent to Princess Road, by dairy worker and future actor, Bruce Jones. His first thoughts upon seeing Jean's body were that she was a disused shop mannequin. The force of the hammer had rendered her unrecognisable, her body mutilated in horrific ways; the most notable was the fact that her neck had been severed by a shard, later recognised as having been carried out days after she was murdered. Sutcliffe had returned back to the body, according to his confession after his arrest in 1981, he realised that the £5 note he had given her for her services could be traced back to him:

> The hammer I used that night was the one I had found lying in my garage after I had taken over my house. I took the hammer back with me. Having driven half way back I realised suddenly that this didn't put me in the clear because I had given her from my wage packet a brand new five pound note. I was working at Clarks then. I was in a dilema [sic] once again. I kept on driving towards home I didn't realise whether she would be found or not. I decided I could not risk going back to retrieve my £5 note and I carried on home.

Sutcliffe had reason to be concerned about the note he had given to Jean. The note found in her handbag five days after her body was discovered was one from a new batch of notes that had been put into his wage packet in the days before he had encountered Jean and bore a particular serial number that the bank of England could confirm was only part of a consignment that had only been sent to two branches of Midland Bank– Shipley and Bingley. Further investigations would show that this particular note had been sent in a large stack to a sub-branch just outside of Bradford just a few days before Jean's murder, which had subsequently been split up and distributed into the wage packets of various local businesses on Thursday 29th September and also Friday 30th September. Unbeknownst to Sutcliffe, police began to track down each individual paid in the area over those two days.

> I was puzzled when no mention of this was made in the Newspapers or TV over the next few days. I decided before a week was out that she was lying there undiscovered and that I would go back to retrieve the £5 note. One night about a week later the opportunity arose for me to go back as we were

having a house warming party with family and gathering the coming weekend. My mother and father brothers and sisters came from Bingley to my house and at the end of the party I ran them home then I made my return trip to Manchester This was about 11pm on either the Saturday or Sunday. I drove to the allotments in my red Corsair and arrived there within 45 minutes.

It would be recorded by police and later confirmed by Sutcliffe that Jean had been killed in the allotment, her clothing stripped away and her body concealed by a heavy door from a nearby shed. Her killer had then returned to the scene and in a vicious rage at not being able to find the bag or the note had stabbed her eight times in the chest, stomach and lower regions. When Sutcliffe had returned and mutilated her body, he had also attempted to decapitate her. Police did not officially link her murder until May 1978. During this time Sutcliffe was interviewed four times by police about the £5 note, after they had traced it back to the lorry firm he worked for. Unfortunately for Sutcliffe's victims and the police, they would let him walk without suspicion.

Marilyn Moore's attack took place on Prince Phillip Playing Field, where Sutcliffe had killed Wilma two years previously. Unlike Wilma, Marilyn would survive. This attack, carried out at around 8.30 pm, was intercepted when Marilyn's screams from the hammer blows prompted dogs in the area to bark. Sutcliffe sped off in his car, leaving Marilyn for dead. She managed to reach the main road and call for help. While her description of her attacker was a credible likeness, she described him as having a Liverpool accent.

Throughout the year of 1977 Sutcliffe killed four women and at least two of the murders are of notable importance to the idea that Sutcliffe could be responsible for Judith's murder when you look at the changing MO and the similarities to earlier attacks. By the end of

January 1978, the police's enquiry team wondered if the serial killer responsible for attacking and killing women in the north had been scared off by the aborted attempt on Marilyn Moore. What they did not know at the time was that he had killed again. The body would not be found for some time. Yvonne Pearson was killed on 21 January 1978, although her body would not be found until Easter Sunday (26 March 1978). Sutcliffe picked Yvonne up from Lumb Lane, a known area for sex workers at the time, before driving her to the back of Drummond's Mill, where his father worked. Here, Sutcliffe set about his vicious attack on Yvonne. On this occasion Sutcliffe had used a large headed lump hammer to deliver the massive head blows inflicted. This was to cause some confusion to the police when her body was found; causing them to wrongly believe that a large stone had been used by the killer. The blows to Yvonne's skull did not immediately kill her and Sutcliffe was startled when another driver parked up close to his car. In an attempt to disguise his crime, he covered Yvonne's body with a heavy sofa to muffle her groans, he also grabbed handfuls of horsehair from the same sofa and rammed the fibres down Yvonne's throat, all the while holding her nose to suffocate her and finish the job he had started. Yvonne was a fighter, and despite this brutal attack she was still alive, causing Sutcliffe to attempt to suffocate her for a second time when he realised that he had not been successful.

The car that had startled him had left the scene and Sutcliffe was left alone with a near-dead Yvonne. He pulled her trousers down and exposed her breasts. While Yvonne lay totally vulnerable and in pain, Sutcliffe began kicking her in the body and her already caved in skull. Still not satisfied he jumped up and down on her chest before covering her body with soil, rubble, and turf. The shallow makeshift grave was then covered by the same sofa he had used earlier to conceal her body. Although he subsequently denied it, Sutcliffe had returned to the scene exactly one month after the murder to make her body more visible, and had placed a copy of the *Daily Mirror* newspaper dated 21 February 1978 under one of her arms, in order to make it look as though she had been murdered then. On 26 March 1978, Yvonne's decomposing body was found on wasteland off Lumb Lane in Bradford by a passer-by who had noticed her arm sticking out from under an old sofa. The fact that she had been bludgeoned to death with a large blunt instrument presumed to have been a rock caused police to wonder that this was not the usual method of their elusive killer, but many features of this murder were similar to other deaths attributed to him.

Ten days later, 18-year-old Helen Rytka was picked up by Sutcliffe on 31 January 1978, in Huddersfield, while Yvonne's body continued to be concealed on the ground of Drummond's Mill.

Helen was a twin sister to Rita, who she lived with, and a sibling to another sister and brother. Writings on Helen paint a picture of a girl with a warm heart, beautiful singing voice and a broken childhood, having been in the care system for a number of years with her siblings before moving to Huddersfield at the end of 1977; at first alone, but later accompanied by Rita. She had only been living in Huddersfield a few weeks before she was murdered. Newspapers will normally and unfairly refer to Helen as a 'good time girl', a phrase of the time relating to anyone who was not a stereotypical housewife tucked up in a home caring for their husband and children. A phrase often used when describing Sutcliffe's victims. They were either 'good time girls' or 'innocent victims' according to news reports. Never both.

In the car with Helen, Sutcliffe claims that the young woman, who had been working part-time as a sex worker along with her twin sister Rita for the past few weeks, began to arouse him 'against his wishes' and that he pulled the car over into the yard of Garrard's Timber Yard on Great Northern Street, under the pretence of needing to urinate. He was unable to but ordered Helen into the back of the car. As she turned to get in, Sutcliffe went to strike her across the head with a hammer. Sutcliffe's weapon struck down on the car instead, only slightly catching Helen's head, causing her to believe Sutcliffe had struck her with his left hand. However the swipe had spooked her, and Sutcliffe, noticing that there were a couple of taxis only some 40 yards or so in the distance, realised he could be caught, but it did nothing to deter his plan to kill Helen. He pushed her down in front of the car and put his hand over her mouth to keep her from screaming. While he had her in this position, Sutcliffe forced himself on her. In his disgusting explanation given to police after his capture in 1981, he stated:

> I had no alternative than to go ahead with the act of sex as the only means thereby of persuading her to keep quiet, as I had already dropped the hammer several yards away.

After he had climaxed, he noticed that the taxis had gone and quickly grabbed for the hammer.

Helen must have seen this as a chance to flee past him but she was unlucky, as she tried to dash past Sutcliffe and between him and the car he swung at her head with the hammer, this time, his aim was true. Sutcliffe later confessed that after dragging Helen back to the front of the car, which concealed him from view he

> took the knife from the front of the car and stabbed her several times in the heart and the lungs. After this, I pulled her to a place a few yards away where I thought she wouldn't be found so quickly, when I got there I covered her with a sheet of asbestos or corrugated metal.

Helen's body was found on the afternoon of Friday, 3 February 1978, wedged into a tight space of no more than 18 inches.

The savagery of Helen's murder, along with all the other cold-blooded attacks that Sutcliffe carried out, is a brutal display of the characteristics of a seriously deranged individual. What is also a potential clue to tie Judith to the 1978 victim is that not only was Helen only 18, one of the youngest of the confirmed victims, but her body was concealed with a sheet of corrugated asbestos by Sutcliffe – remember, Judith's body had been hidden beneath a sheet of corrugated asbestos too in Robinson's Field. Helen had severe injuries to her head and she was around Judith's age too, born in 1959.

The last woman killed in 1978 was 40-year-old Vera Millward. On Tuesday, 16 May 1978 she was driven by Sutcliffe to the grounds of Manchester Royal Infirmary for solicitation; again an attack carried out beyond the realms of West Yorkshire. While she was in the car with Sutcliffe he attacked her with a hammer. Vera tried to fight him off but Sutcliffe was armed and at this stage had significant experience in killing, Vera didn't stand a chance. Her screams echoed through the cold winter air, heard by a man walking in the area close to the hospital, and then stopped. He assumed it was coming from the hospital. Heavy blows to the head killed Vera, but after her death, Sutcliffe dragged her lifeless corpse to a spot by the fence in the carpark and proceeded to stab her with a knife. She was found at 8.00 am the following morning.

Sutcliffe went on to kill two more women the following year. On Wednesday, 4 April 1979 Sutcliffe struck again, this time in Halifax after travelling some 260 miles for T&S Clark's transport. Josephine Whitaker aged 19 years old, a building society clerk, left her grandparents' house well after 11.00 pm to take the ten minute walk home. It was almost midnight when she reached Savile Park Moor, an open area of grassland surrounded by well-lit roads. As she walked across the damp grass in the park, Sutcliffe stopped her to ask the time. She looked towards the town clock in the distance and he took a hammer out of his jacket, smashing it down on the young woman's head. As she lay on the grass, he hit her again and then dragged her 30 feet back into the darkness away from the road. He pulled her clothing back and stabbed her twenty-five times into her breasts, stomach, thighs and vagina. He left her lying like a bundle of rags. One of her tan shoes still laid at the roadside where his attack had begun. She had almost been in sight of her home when he had killed her.

Josephine was found at 6.30 am the next morning by a woman going to a bus stop. Around the same time Josephine's younger brother was setting off to the newsagents for his early morning paper round, and as he neared the park, he saw police officers huddled around something lying near the roadside and then recognised his sister's shoe. He went home in a state and, upon checking, found Josephine's bedroom empty and called the police.

Scenes of crime officers found the same size 7 Wellington boot prints at this scene as in the previous crime scenes of Patricia Atkinson and Emily Jackson and discovered that the right impression was worn more than the left, suggesting a lorry driver. The pathologist's report revealed that there had been traces of milling oil and metal particles found in the victim's wounds which suggested an engineering connection. When we revisit Judith's murder and the pathology report from Dr van der Merwe and the 'series of parallel stabbing-type injuries' that were 'inflicted on the left temple area fragmenting the underlying bone' we note that a very similar frenzied stabbing attack was carried out on Josephine by Sutcliffe, who used a specially adapted Phillips screwdriver which he later told police he had discarded down a motorway embankment near the M1.

Detectives later retrieved the rusty long screwdriver, which had been sharpened before the attack. Instead of the normal 'X' mark, which a normal Phillips screwdriver made, this adaptation left a 'Y' mark. At Sutcliffe's 1981 trial, Sir Michael Havers commented:

> It was done in a way to make it what you may think is one of the most fiendish weapons you have ever seen.

Commenting on the murder of Josephine Whitaker, Havers said:

> Josephine's skull was fractured from ear to ear. She had been stabbed twenty-one times in the trunk, six times in the right leg. Her vagina had been stabbed three times in the awful way of using the same entry each time.

The screwdriver, which was passed around to members of the jury, had also been used in Barbara Leach's murder. Sutcliffe told police:

> I used it on Josephine Whitaker and Barbara Leach. It was a giant Phillips screwdriver which was badly worn and had been converted into a bradawl.

Barbara Leach, 20, was attacked in Bradford on 2 September 1979. From Kettering, Barbara was a student at the University of Bradford. On the evening she was attacked, she left her digs in Grove Terrace just across Great Horton Road from the university and went to The Mannville Arms pub situated at 31–33 Great Horton Road with five of her friends. Barbara and her friends stayed behind to help clean up and had a drink with the landlord and they left at 12.45 am, nearly two hours later.

Sutcliffe was driving through the area and was watching nearby as they walked down Great Horton Road. Barbara decided to go for a walk and left the group, walking away from them, up Great Horton Road towards the university. Sutcliffe drove his car to Ashgrove where he parked the car and, armed with a hammer and knife in hand, got out of the car and walked quickly along the alleyway at the rear called Back Ashgrove knowing that Barbara would soon be walking past at the other end. He waited in the shadows, listening to the echo of her boots on the pavement as she approached and, as she passed by, he sprang – smashing the hammer into her head, it only took one blow to kill her. Both these women were of a similar age to Helen and Judith, Josephine was born in 1960, Barbara in 1959.

In the final year before he was apprehended, Sutcliffe attacked five more women that we know of, killing two of them. The first known attack and murder of 1980 was 47-year-old Marguerite Walls, who was killed in Farnsley on Wednesday, 20 August 1980. Her body was covered with grass cuttings and leaves. The partial hiding of the body in Marguerite Walls's case had earlier been mirrored in Yvonne's and Helen's murders: Yvonne being covered with a sofa and Helen with corrugated metal, a clear pattern and distinctive characteristic in a serial killer. Sutcliffe's second known victim of the year was Dr Upadhya Bandara, 34 years old, attacked by Sutcliffe on Wednesday, 24 September 1980 in Leeds.

A month later, Maureen 'Mo' Lea, a 20-year-old third-year student at University of Leeds became the third woman attacked by Sutcliffe in what would be his final year of freedom, the night of 25 October 1980, but she managed to survive after passerby Lorna Smith interrupted the attack.

Theresa Sykes, 16, was attacked on Wednesday, 5 November 1980 in Huddersfield. She also survived, again but a mere child out in the world who Sutcliffe targeted.

The final victim of Sutcliffe's slayings was 20-year-old student Jaqueline Hill who was killed in Leeds on Monday, 17 November 1980.

The evidence against Sutcliffe stacks up when you look at the patterns of his victims – certainly not without some form of smarts, he evaded police, in part, due to his ability to spot an opportunity and know how to hide in plain sight. He would change his MO ever so slightly every few months, changes that would often mean that police did not immediately link the victim or the survivor to him. There is evidence that women like Anna, Olive and Wilma were not his first victims, looking at his 1969 'stone in sock' incident. There is also evidence that Sutcliffe travelled outside of West Yorkshire and had the means to do so, like with the murder of Barbara Leach where records show he travelled approximately 260 miles in a day and, despite the outdated and narrow minded view that Sutcliffe only attacked and killed sex workers, clearly the age and occupation of his victims was not the clincher for him – sex workers were and have been for decades, vulnerable targets for the depravity of people like Sutcliffe. He was merely an opportunist.

Talk to any West Yorkshire Police officer who served in the late 1970s and early 1980s, and most, if not all, will say that the detective work carried out in these eras, unaccompanied by computers or DNA and forensics the way we know it today, was their best work. Indeed, the detectives tasked with catching Sutcliffe were under an unreal amount of pressure and desperate to identify this maniac before he struck again, each and every new murder case flaunting the killer's deviance in their faces and their 'incompetence' in the face of the public. Police across the country had dealt with serial killers, but what Sutcliffe was doing was undeniably different and his deviance all the more twisted, even if just measured by the sheer volume of his victims. The *Aberdeen Evening Press* wrote on 19 May 1979, approximately twenty months before he was caught:

> As elusive as Jack the Ripper, he has proved more callous and calculating than the Black Panther Donald Neilson, and more systematically sadistic than the moors murderers Ian Brady and Myra Hindley.

Police finally caught up with Sutcliffe in January 1981. At his trial that same year, James Armstrong Chadwin, for the defence, said to Sutcliffe:

> How were you during the period 1969 to 1975 yourself?

Sutcliffe replied:

> Just the same, I suffered from depression. I came to live in London for a year and then went to work on nights because I didn't like carrying on with the mission and I was in turmoil a great deal of the time.

In reply to a question from the judge Mr Justice Boreham, Sutcliffe stated he went to live in London for a year in 1970 while Sonia was at the McMillan Teacher Training College in Deptford, but before she finished her teacher training course in 1972, he returned to Bradford during autumn 1971 and got a job at Baird Television in Lidget Green.

Chadwin asked Sutcliffe whether between the years 1969 and 1975 he had any doubts in his mind or asked himself about the mission. Sutcliffe replied:

> Yes. Why it should be me that did it because I found it so difficult. When I went to live in London, I saw Sonia practically all the time and it never had a chance to get on top of me. Then I went to work nights for about three years and this kept me busy every night, and at weekends I saw Sonia, so I was able to overcome it.

Of somewhat great importance, Sutcliffe had access to various modes of transport: either a lorry, his Morris 1000 or the Ford Escort belonging to Mrs Szurma, his future mother-in-law. Let's not also forget that Sutcliffe has shown he is not above attempting to break into a vehicle, his 1965 conviction for attempted theft. While Sutcliffe was roaming the streets, another man would come to sit in prison for killing Judith, a crime he did not commit. A crime we now know could potentially be linked to Sutcliffe.

Chapter Six

A Scapegoat

Among their routine enquiries into Judith's murder, Staffordshire Police interviewed soldiers who were serving at Whittington Barracks. One was former boy soldier Andrew James Evans, a 17-year-old soldier who, having suffered an asthma attack, was awaiting discharge on medical grounds. On 7 June 1972, the evening Judith Roberts was killed, he was a day away from handing in his uniform and returning home, travelling approximately 40 miles away to Longton, near Newcastle-under-Lyme, to live with his grandmother, Irene.

A semi-literate, anxious and socially awkward teenager, a search into Evans' past would show his character to be of a good nature. The boy was born Andrew James Evans on 18 April 1955 in Stafford to his parents, Joan and Bill. He was one of four children – the second eldest, he had a brother and two sisters. He received a secondary school education at schools in the Burton-on-Trent area. School reports signed by his headmaster showed that although he was of limited ability, Evans tried hard in school and was helpful, reliable and never in trouble. He was immature and chose companions of a similar nature. Since leaving school Evans was known to have worked as a trainee printer shop assistant and trainee machinist for employers in the Burton-on-Trent area. As his headmaster had described him, Evans' employers also found him to be of good character and a good timekeeper. In April 1972, he enlisted in the Gloucestershire Regiment, but was dismissed on 15 June 1972 as he ceased to fulfil army medical requirements. Evans fell into a period of unemployment until August 1972.

On 31 August 1972, he commenced work as an agent for a brush company, selling products door to door. His sales were very poor, and he only received a total of £4.50 for five weeks' employment. This employment terminated when he was taken into custody. He had joined the armed forces in the hope of a career but alas, his condition was largely debilitating. After his discharge he was treated for depression, and prescribed Valium for that condition. It is worth noting that Evans had no prior convictions before he was questioned about Judith's murder.

As part of the police investigation into the murder, soldiers residing at Whittington Barracks on 7 June 1972 were required to complete a form giving an account of their whereabouts for that evening, providing references. Evans said that he had spent that evening at the barracks, giving the names of three other soldiers who could verify his presence there. However, police subsequently failed to trace one of the named soldiers and discovered the remaining two had left the barracks prior to 7 June 1972.

On 8 October 1972, DCS Saunders and DCS Wright questioned Evans again after having visited him at his grandmother's house. The morning after that interview, Evans told his grandmother that he planned to visit the police station because he wished to see a picture of Judith. The reason for this being that Evans had seen the girl in his dreams, 'a hazy combination of images of women's faces', which convinced him he was the killer. Although his grandmother advised him against such action, he subsequently presented himself to officers at Longton Police Station in a distressed state, where he made his request, telling them he had dreamt of Judith:

> I keep seeing a face. I want to see a picture of her. I wonder if I've done it.

Police, vigilantly hunting Judith's killer, would have had no option but to take his confession seriously.

Sitting down with detectives in a series of interviews, Evans set in motion a course that would change his life in dramatic ways. Face to face with the police he 'confessed'. Evans told detectives that he had dragged Judith from her bicycle, then struggled with her in a field. Asked if he was the killer, he answered:

> This is it. I don't know. Show me a picture and I'll tell you if I've seen it.

Investigators also asked him whether he had ever visited Tamworth, to which he replied:

> I don't know. I don't know. I could have been. I forget where I have been.

Evans was clearly in a distressed state and was without appropriate representation despite his age. His 'confession' was a promising lead. However, detectives initially did not believe his account, dismissing him as a fantasist, but over the three-day period in which Evans was questioned they became increasingly certain Evans was the killer.

Psychologists and Evans' own defence team would later argue that Evans was suffering from hysterical amnesia. 'Amnesia' is a general term that describes memory loss. The loss can be temporary or permanent, but 'amnesia' usually refers to the temporary variety. Causes include head and brain injuries, certain drugs, alcohol, traumatic events or conditions such as Alzheimer's disease. However, the prosecution argued that Evans had sketched the murder scene, the girl's body and the murder weapon and argued that he had provided details of the murder that only the real killer would know.

Now we will examine each stage of how Evans became embroiled in this horrendous crime and became a victim himself of the system, which is supposed to be fair and beyond any shadow of doubt about an accused person's guilt.

> It is better that ten guilty persons escape than that one innocent suffer.
>
> Sir William Blackstone, 1765

Some four months after Judith's murder and with the police no nearer to solving it, they must have thought that their stalled investigation had turned a corner when a confession was forthcoming.

Chapter Seven

The Police Interviews

Extracts from an interview, held on Tuesday, 9 October 1972, by DC Kenneth Peach (of Longton Police Station, Stoke-on-Trent) and DS Roy Williamson (of Hanley Police Station, Staffordshire) with Andrew Evans:

DS Williamson: 'At 9pm on Sunday 8 October 1972 I visited 68 Upper Normacot Road, Longton, Stoke-on-Trent with Detective Constable Peach. To the accused Andrew James Evans "We are police officers engaged on the enquiry into the murder of Judith Roberts which happened at Tamworth on 7 June. You were previously seen by a police officer from Longton who completed a proforma as to your whereabouts during the evening of 7 June. You told him that you had been with Private Fisher, Pearson and Horton. That has been checked out and we now know that Fisher and Pearson left the barracks on 6 June to go to York on a physical development course. The man Horton does not exist. Can you remember what you were doing on 7 June and if possible, who you were with?"'

Andrew Evans: 'That's right Fisher and Pearson did go to the PDC [pre-departure clearance] on the 6th. I remember that but there was someone else there in the barrack room before I left the army on the 8th.'

DC Peach: 'Are you sure it was Horton and not someone with a similar name?'

Andrew Evans: 'It could be Johnson or something like that.'

DC Peach: 'Are you sure you left the army on 8th June? I seem to recall that we have about the 15th of June when you left the army.'

Andrew Evans: 'I'm sure of what date I left because I've got my discharge papers somewhere. I'll try to find them.'

According to the police officers' statement, Evans then spent some considerable time searching the living room and then upstairs. When he came downstairs, he had the discharge certificate, which he handed to DC Peach. By this time Evans appeared quite agitated. He was sweating and appeared very shaky. DS Williamson asked Andrews: 'Are you alright?' To which his grandmother replied on his behalf:

> He suffers with his nerves when he is spoken to. He gets excited and it brings on his asthma.

Evans took a tablet and within a very short time calmed down. It was at this point that Staffordshire Police would have become aware that they were dealing with a vulnerable young man who had mental health issues and should have set in place the safeguards under the Mental Health Act 1959. However, their interrogations continued:

DC Peach: 'This discharge paper clearly states that you left the army on 15th June 1974 and yet you say you left on the 8th.'

Andrew Evans: 'I remember leaving the army on the 8th it was a Thursday. That paper came to me through the post.'

DS Williamson: 'The 15th of June was also a Thursday. Are you sure you left on the 8th of June?'

Andrew Evans: 'It was a Thursday morning; it may have been the 15th.'

DS Williamson: 'As we were leaving the house, Evans accompanied us to the front door.'

DC Peach: 'We shall be making further enquiries at the barracks to try and confirm your story of being in the barracks, and possibly in the NAFFI during the evening of 7th June.'

Andrew Evans: 'What would happen to anyone who did a thing like that?'

DS Williamson: 'He would be in some considerable trouble apart from wanting his bloody head looking into by a psychiatrist.'

While on remand, Evans would later recall of the first two interviews in his defence statement:

The Police first came to see me in September. It was just a routine call to find out where I had been on the evening of June 7th. I told them that I had been at Whittington Barracks and that I had been with Pearson and Fisher, who were two people in the same platoon. I also gave them fingerprints. I thought nothing of it at the time, in fact I thought it was hilarious that they should think that I might have done it.
    The police came again to interview me again one Sunday evening while I was still staying at my grandmothers [*sic*]. They gave me no warning that they were coming. When they arrived, they said I had made a mistake in my statement and that I wasn't away and they had to put it right to keep their

records in order. They said that they had found out that on the Wednesday evening Pearson and Fisher were no longer on the Barracks, so I could not have been with them. I thought a bit about this. I then remembered that Pearson and Fisher had left the morning before I did so that I could not have been with them on my last night in Barracks. I was still sure that I had left on the Wednesday, but they said as far as they knew it had been the Thursday morning that I had left the Barracks.

I was getting a bit worried because I could not remember the day on which I left, so I said I'd go and get my discharge papers. I rushed upstairs to find them but I couldn't find them anywhere. I made them some coffee and then had another look and eventually I found it. It took me about half an hour to find it altogether. The form that I found showed the discharge date as being the 15th, which was at the end of the leave that I had after I had left the Barracks, but it did not show the date on which I had actually left the Barracks.

I then made a statement to them saying that I would have been in either the Barrack Room or the Naafi on the evening of June 7th if I was still in the Barracks. I never went off the Barracks in the evening. I never used to bother to get a Pass. The Police then left. One of these said that everybody made mistakes at some time and that I probably wouldn't be hearing anymore from them. I started getting worried because I couldn't remember what I had been doing on the Wednesday evening. But I was more worried about the fact that I could not remember what I had been doing than about the possibility that I might have killed anybody. I thought that if I could not remember what I had been doing then it was possible that I might have killed somebody, but I did not feel as though I was personally responsible for killing anyone.

When I went to bed that night I kept waking up with nightmares. I kept seeing this youngish face which was rather like my sister, Sandra. The face kept appearing. I remember seeing odd shapes forming into a face. I had the dream two or three times and I woke up because of it. When I woke up in the morning, I did not know whose face it was, but I think now that it may have been my sisters [sic]. At first the face did not worry me, and then I started thinking about what had happened the day before, and I thought that maybe I had done it. I am pretty good at putting two and two together and it seemed possible that I could have done it. During the morning, I remember saying to my grandmother 'I may have done that you know.' She told me not to be stupid. I don't think I went to work that morning. After lunch my grandmother was going to have a rest. I said that I was going down to the police station to ask to see a picture because I thought I may have done it. After she had gone to sleep, I went down to the Police station at Longton. I went in. I had been feeling ill all morning. I was feeling sick and I was shaking because I was worried about the face that I had seen in my dream. When I got in the police station, I told them my name and said that I had been asked to give a statement about the Tamworth murder, and then I said that I had got asthma and I broke down. I was feeling so bad. I was crying. I kept trying to impress on them that I had asthma and that any nervous state would bring on an attack. The Sergeant behind the desk kept saying that it was a CID matter. I can't remember a lot about what happened after that but I don't think that I was questioned by Longton Police.

An extract from the statement of Paul Cooper, a police cadet stationed at Longton Police Station:

During Monday 9th October 1972 I was engaged on Charge Office duty in plain clothes at the police station. At about 3pm that day there was a knock on the enquiry window. I answered the window and I saw a young lad wearing spectacles. Before I said anything to him he said to me.

Andrew Evans: 'I'd like to see the CID.'

Paul Cooper: 'What for?'

Andrew Evans: 'Two CID blokes called on me last night, I am very nervous, can I see them?'

Paul Cooper: 'As the boy spoke I noticed that his body was shaking and he was stuttering when speaking. I asked the boy what he wanted to see the CID for.'

Andrew Evans: 'I want to see a picture of the girl in the Tamworth murder, I am very nervous, I suffer from nerves, I keep dreaming about this girl, I have just come out of the Army.'

Paul Cooper: 'I then walked him across to the CID General Office where I spoke to Detective Sergeant [Ernest] Dinsdale. After speaking to DS Dinsdale I called the boy into the office. He was still very nervous and shaking.'

DS Dinsdale to Andrew Evans: 'What do you want?'

Andrew Evans: 'I want to see a photograph of the girl.'

DS Dinsdale: 'What for?'

Andrew Evans: 'Two CID men came to see me last night.'

Paul Cooper: 'The boy then took a few paces forward towards a desk, laid his hands outstretched on the desk and lowered his head and began crying and sobbing heavily and loudly. Det Sgt Dinsdale placed a chair underneath the boy and told him to sit down I then left the CID office.'

DS Dinsdale to Andrew Evans: 'Sit down son, calm yourself.'

DS Dinsdale: 'Evans sat down on the chair. He was still crying. He was leaning forward with his head between his knees and his hands on his face. He continued crying and was left alone to calm down. After about two minutes he became more composed and stopped sobbing, although he was still crying. I said to him "Now what do you want?"'

Andrew Evans: 'I want to talk to them two men who came last night. I want to see a photograph of the girl. I was in the Army, I don't remember where I was.'

DS Dinsdale: 'Detective Inspector Houlston and Detective Constable Bowyer were present and approached me and the boy, and I said to them in his presence. "He wants to talk about the Tamworth murder." They both left the General Office with him and went upstairs to the Detective Inspector's Office.'

We strongly believe that at this point the formal interviewing of Evans began and he should either have been arrested and cautioned or told that he was free to leave the police station if he wished. Neither occurred in the sworn statements of the police officers involved.

Extracts of statements made by DI Keith Houlston and DC Charles Bowyer:

> DI Houlston: 'I asked DC Bowyer to bring the boy to my office and Evans sat down on a chair in front of my desk next to DC Bowyer. I sat at my desk and Evans was still crying and appeared to be very nervous.'
>
> DC Bowyer: 'What's your name and where do you live?'
>
> Andrew Evans: 'Andrew Evans, 68 Upper Normacot Road.'
>
> DI Houlston: 'Who lives with you?'
>
> Andrew Evans: 'Me [my] gran.'
>
> DC Bowyer: 'Where are your parents?'
>
> Andrew Evans: 'We don't get on. They live at Burton.'
>
> DC Bowyer: 'What is the trouble? Why are you so upset?'
>
> Andrew Evans: 'It is this girl who was murdered at Tamworth. I keep seeing a face. I wonder if I've done it.'
>
> DI Houlston: 'Can you describe this face?'
>
> Andrew Evans: Nine inches long, dark hair, darkish eyes, chubby face, not too chubby, wearing a dress.
>
> DI Houlston: 'What colour dress?'

Andrew Evans: 'Flowers on it.'

DI Houlston: 'How old was she? Do you think?'

Andrew Evans: 'About fourteen. Why do I keep seeing this face?'

DC Bowyer: 'Do you think you've done it?'

DI Houlston: 'At this point Evans clenched his fists at each side of his head and [Andrew Evans] said "I don't know whether I've done it or not. I know I was in the Army and I left on the Wednesday."'

DI Houlston: 'You were in the army where?'

Andrew Evans: 'Whittington [Barracks].'

DI Houlston: 'When did you leave?'

Andrew Evans: 'On the Wednesday I think.'

DI Houlston: 'What date?'

Andrew Evans: 'The 7th or 8th of June. Here's my discharge paper.'

DI Houlston: 'Evans handed me an Army Discharge Form (later labelled KPH 1).'

DI Houlston: 'Why did you leave?'

Andrew Evans: 'Medical grounds I've got Asthma.'

DI Houlston: 'This says the 15th June.'

Andrew Evans: 'I know, that came through the post some days after and I knew straight away it was the wrong date, I left about a week before.'

DI Houlston: 'Do you know where the murder was?'

Andrew Evans: 'Tamworth.'

DI Houlston: 'Have you ever been to Tamworth?'

Andrew Evans: 'I don't know I don't know I could have done. I forget where I've been. I've been down streets and in houses and later I wonder how I got there.'

DC Bowyer: 'What time were you discharged?'

Andrew Evans: 'About midday.'

DC Bowyer: 'Where did you go when you left the Barracks?'

Andrew Evans: 'I turned right towards Lichfield and got a lift in a car. This dropped me off in Lichfield by the bus station opposite the railway station isn't it?'

DI Houlston: 'Then where did you go?'

Andrew Evans: 'I caught a bus to Burton. I went to see me mum. I don't know what time I got there.'

DC Bowyer: 'Who was in the house when you got there?'

Andrew Evans: 'Just my mother. I know I left about 5pm because my brother had not come home from work. You see I can't remember. This is how I am. I could have got home the next day. I don't know where I've been. This is why I keep wondering if it's me that's done this murder. Can you show me a picture to see if I've ever met her?'

DI Houlston: 'What happened at home?'

Andrew Evans: 'We had an argument.'

DI Houlston: 'What about?'

Andrew Evans: 'Just a family bother.'

DC Bowyer: 'Where did you go after you left home?'

Andrew Evans: 'I can't really remember.'

DC Bowyer: 'What time did you get to your gran's?'

Andrew Evans: 'I can't really remember.'

DI Houlston: 'Have you done this murder?'

At this point, under the Judges' Rules, DI Houlston should have cautioned Evans. The rules did not alter the law on admissibility of evidence but became a code of best practice; it was assumed that statements given by a suspect in accordance with the Judges' Rules would be admissible in evidence.

***

Judges' Rules 1912

The Judges' Rules were first established in 1912 to provide police forces with guidance on procedures. The Judges' Rules were, at that time, as follows:

1. Allowed the police to question any person with a view to finding out whether, or by whom, an offence had been committed.
2. Required the police to give a caution when they had evidence to suspect that a person had committed an offence.
3. Required a further caution when a person was charged and prohibited questioning afterwards charging save in exceptional circumstances.
4. Required a record of questioning to be kept.
5. Gave guidance on the best way to record a formal written statement.
6. The rules also included administrative guidance on access to defence counsel, and on questioning children and foreigners.

Judges' Rules 1918

Five further rules were added to the original four Judges' Rules in 1918, and the rules were further explained in 1934 in a Home Office Circular 536053/23. The Judges' Rules were updated again in 1964 as Practice Note (Judges' Rules) (1964) 1 WLR 152, so the updated Judges' Rules were in force at the time of Judith Roberts's death. The Judges' Rules formulated in 1912 and 1918 read as follows:

1. When a police officer is endeavouring to discover the author of a crime, there is no objection to them putting questions in respect thereof to any person or persons, whether suspected or not, from

whom they think that useful information can be obtained. R. versus Cook (1959) 2 All E.R. 97.
2. Whenever a police officer has made up their mind to charge a person with a crime, they should first caution such a person before asking any questions or further questions, as the case may be.
3. Persons in custody should not be questioned without the usual caution being first administered.
4. If the prisoner wishes to volunteer a statement, the usual caution should be administered. It is advisable that the last two words (i.e. 'against you') of the usual caution should be omitted and end with the words 'be given in evidence.'
5. The caution to be administered to a prisoner, when they are formally charged, should be in the following words:

> Do you wish to say anything in answer to the charge? You are not obliged to say anything unless you wish to do so, but whatever you say will be taken down in writing and may be given in evidence.

6. A statement by a prisoner before there is time to caution them is not rendered inadmissible in evidence merely by reason of no caution having been given, but in such a case they should be cautioned as soon as possible.
7. A prisoner making a voluntary statement must not be cross-examined, and no questions should be put to them about it except for the purpose of removing ambiguity in what he has actually said. For instance, if he has mentioned an hour without saying whether it was morning or evening, or has given a day of the week and day of the month which do not agree, or has not made it clear to what individual or what place they intended to refer in some part of his statement, they may be questioned sufficiently to clear up the point.

8. Refers to two or more not relevant in this case.
9. Any statement made in accordance with the above rules should, whenever possible, be taken down in writing and signed by the person making it after it has been read to them and he has been invited to make any corrections he may wish.

Judges' Rule 3 was the rule that generally caused the most comments: What does 'in custody' mean?

This was decided in one case to mean 'in the custody of the police.' But what if the suspect is asked to go to the police station for questioning? Is he in custody?

This again was decided by case law; if a suspect was in a position to refuse to go the police station, they were not in custody and therefore did not have to be cautioned. On the other hand, when a person was interrogated in a room at the police station for three quarters of an hour and the police admitted, at the trial, that if they had tried to leave they would have prevented them, it was held that they were in custody.

***

The interview continues at the point after DI Houlston has asked Evans if he has done the murder.

DI Houlston: 'Have you done this murder?'

Andrew Evans: 'This is it. I don't know. Show me a picture and I'll tell you if I have ever seen her.'

DC Bowyer: 'Have you got or ever had a girlfriend?'

Andrew Evans: 'No I haven't. I've nothing against girls, but I don't bother much. I've only had one date when I was fifteen and that was a disaster.'

DC Bowyer: 'Why was that?'

Andrew Evans: 'The date had been made by somebody else, and I was mistaken for another lad who this girl fancied. This was at Burton-on-Trent. There is a girl I fancy at Normacot Co-Op but she doesn't fancy me.'

DI Houlston: 'Have you got a sister?'

Andrew Evans: 'Yes but she hits me and if I hit her back I get it.'

DI Houlston: 'Is she younger or older?'

Andrew Evans: 'Younger.'

DC Bowyer: 'You've never had sex with a girl?'

Andrew Evans laughed out loud and smiled for the first time and said:

Andrew Evans: 'No. But when I was about thirteen, I remember being with another lad and two girls about the same age and we were lying down when one of the girls, a great big one sat on me and tried to pull my trousers down. The other one sat on my arm but I managed to fight them off and my mate sat laughing at me.'

DI Houlston: 'Right Andrew, I'll make further enquiries about this and perhaps someone from Tamworth will want a word with you'

Andrew Evans: 'Yes alright, but if they want me to go to Tamworth perhaps you'll let my granny know because she'll wonder where I am. She doesn't know I've come here. She's having a nap. I told her I was worried and wanted to see a picture of this girl and was coming down the Police Station but she told me not to be so daft. She doesn't know I've come down here this afternoon.'

DC Bowyer: 'The interview concluded about 3:30pm the same day. Throughout this interview Evans was crying more or less continually. There were short periods when he appeared to be more composed. Detective Inspector Houlston made a telephone call.'

The statement does not indicate what police status Evans was during the time of arrival of the next set of police officers, but it is clear that for the next three quarters of an hour he was in the CID office of Longton Police Station. Whether as a detainee or assisting with police enquiries is not clear but he was not offered any medical attention nor a solicitor or anyone acting on his behalf.

Extracts from statement made by DCI Stanley Wood at police headquarters, Stafford:

DCI Wood: 'At 4:15pm on Monday 9 October 1972 with Detective Constable Peter Colclough I visited Longton Police Station where I saw Andrew James Evans in the CID Office. He was in a very distressed state and having introduced myself I told him to calm down and said, "I understand you want to see someone about the murder at Tamworth?"'

Andrew Evans: 'Yes, I want to see a photograph of the girl who was murdered. I think I killed her.'

DCI Wood: 'Try and calm yourself. This is a very serious matter and you should be quite sure of anything you say. Why do you think you killed her?'

At this point again Evans should have been cautioned.

Andrew Evans: 'I keep seeing her face all the time. I can't sleep I've got to know if I did it because I think I must have done.'

DCI Wood: 'Can you describe the face you see and anything else about her?'

Andrew Evans: 'She's got long straightish hair.'

DCI Wood: 'Is that all you see?'

Andrew Evans: 'No. She's wearing a dress. It's white with something like flowers on it. I must be going mad. I can see her all the time.'

DC Colclough: 'How does she appear when you see her, is she standing up, lying down or what?'

Andrew Evans 'I think she was lying down.'

DC Colclough: 'Have you got a girlfriend. Is it her face you are seeing?'

Andrew Evans: 'No I haven't got one. I've never had one.'

DCI Wood: 'How long have you been in this condition?'

Andrew Evans: 'For a few weeks now. I'm having treatment from the doctor for depression, I have to take tablets every day.'

DCI Wood: 'Is the fact that you think you murdered the girl in Tamworth the reason for your depression or is there some other reason?'

Andrew Evans: 'I'm not very happy with the job I'm doing. I'm a Kleeneze salesman. I can't get anything else. I was in the Army at Whittington Barracks but was discharged on medical grounds. I suffer with asthma.'

DCI Wood: 'At this stage he began to cry bitterly slumped forward in his seat and we decided to take him to another room in the building to allow him to recover. He was so distressed it was necessary to assist him in this room. He was obviously having difficulty due to his asmathatical condition and repeated several times "I must have killed her."'

Evans had in his possession an Army Discharge Certificate indicating that he was discharged from the army on medical grounds on 15th June 1972.

DCI Wood: 'This document shows your discharge from the Army on 15 June 1972. Is this the date you left Whittington Barracks?'

Andrew Evans: 'No. They sent that through the post after I had left. When I left the Barracks they gave me one which was dated 8th June. I remember it was a Wednesday when I left, just after midday. I've mislaid the one they gave me.'

DCI Wood: 'The 8th of June was a Thursday. Do you remember which day it was?'

Andrew Evans: 'I'm sure it was a Wednesday, but I have a bad memory. I can't remember things that have happened even a short while before. I can put my glasses or a book down and soon after I can't remember what I have done with them. It's been like that all my life. What day was the girl murdered?'

DCI Wood: 'I propose to tell you at this stage. If you believe you killed the girl I want you to think very carefully about it.'

Once again, no caution was forthcoming.

Andrew Evans: 'I'm trying to remember, but I can't think of anything else.'

DC Colclough: 'Are you sure there isn't anything else you can remember about the girl?'

Andrew Evans: 'No all I keep doing is seeing her face.'

DCI Wood: 'When you left Whittington Barracks having been discharged, do you remember what you did?'

Andrew Evans: 'Yes I came out of the Guardroom and crossed the road towards Lichfield, it must have been about 2 o'clock because I'd just had a meal a little time before. I crossed the main road towards Lichfield and thumbed a lift, I was standing on the opposite side of the road to the Barracks. A man in a blue car picked me up and dropped me off by the railway station in Lichfield. I wanted to get to Burton to see my Mum.

When I got out of the car I walked straight across the road to the Bus Station which is nearly opposite and caught a bus to Burton. I got to my mum's just after 3 o'clock and left again at about 5 o'clock. There was only my mum there and I wanted to go before anybody else came. I don't get on with my sister she is always on to me.'

DCI Wood: 'What do you mean, you don't get on? How old is she?'

Andrew Evans: 'She's ten, oh no, nine. She's always hitting and kicking me and never leaves me alone.'

DC Colclough: 'What were you wearing when you left the Barracks?'

Andrew Evans: 'The clothes that I's [I am] wearing now.'

DC Colclough: 'Are these the only civilian clothes you've got? What happened to your uniform?'

Andrew Evans: 'These were the only civvies I'd got all the time I was in the Army, and I handed all my uniform in on the morning I left. I'd never been issued with a number one dress; I'd only ever had day uniform and combat kit.'

DCI Wood: 'What did you do when you left your mother's?'

Andrew Evans: 'I wanted to go to my Gran's at Longton. I caught a train at Burton to Derby and then to Uttoxeter. It must have been about nine o'clock when I got to Uttoxeter.

Police search party for Judith Roberts, June 1975. (Mirrorpix)

The entrance to Robinson's Field. (Staffordshire Police)

Cumberford Lane on the outer side of Robinson's Field. (Staffordshire Police)

The site where Judith's body was found. Her prized bike sticks out from the bushes on the right, marking the location where she was found. (Staffordshire Police)

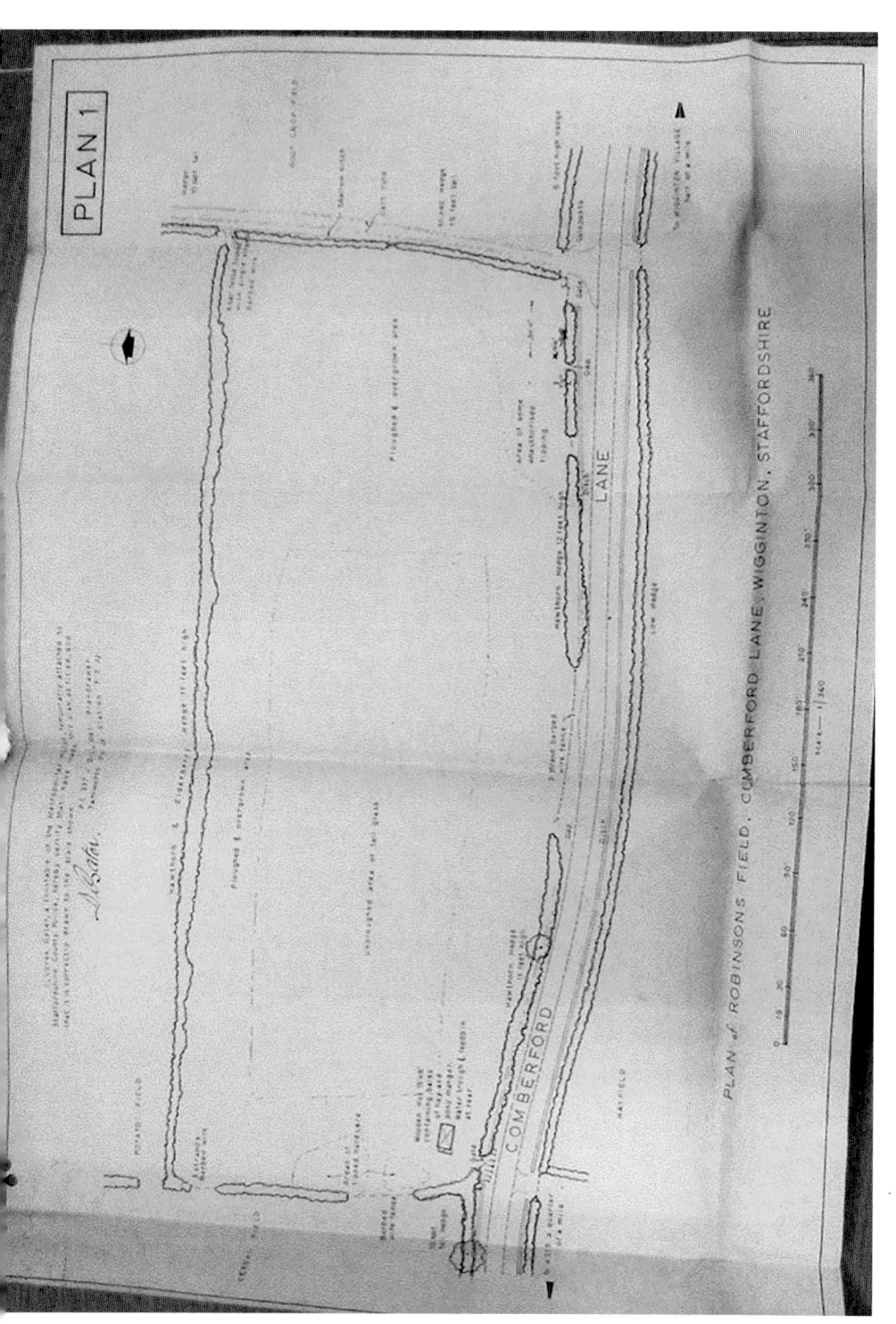

A layout of Robinson's Field. (Andrew Evans' appeal file, The National Archives)

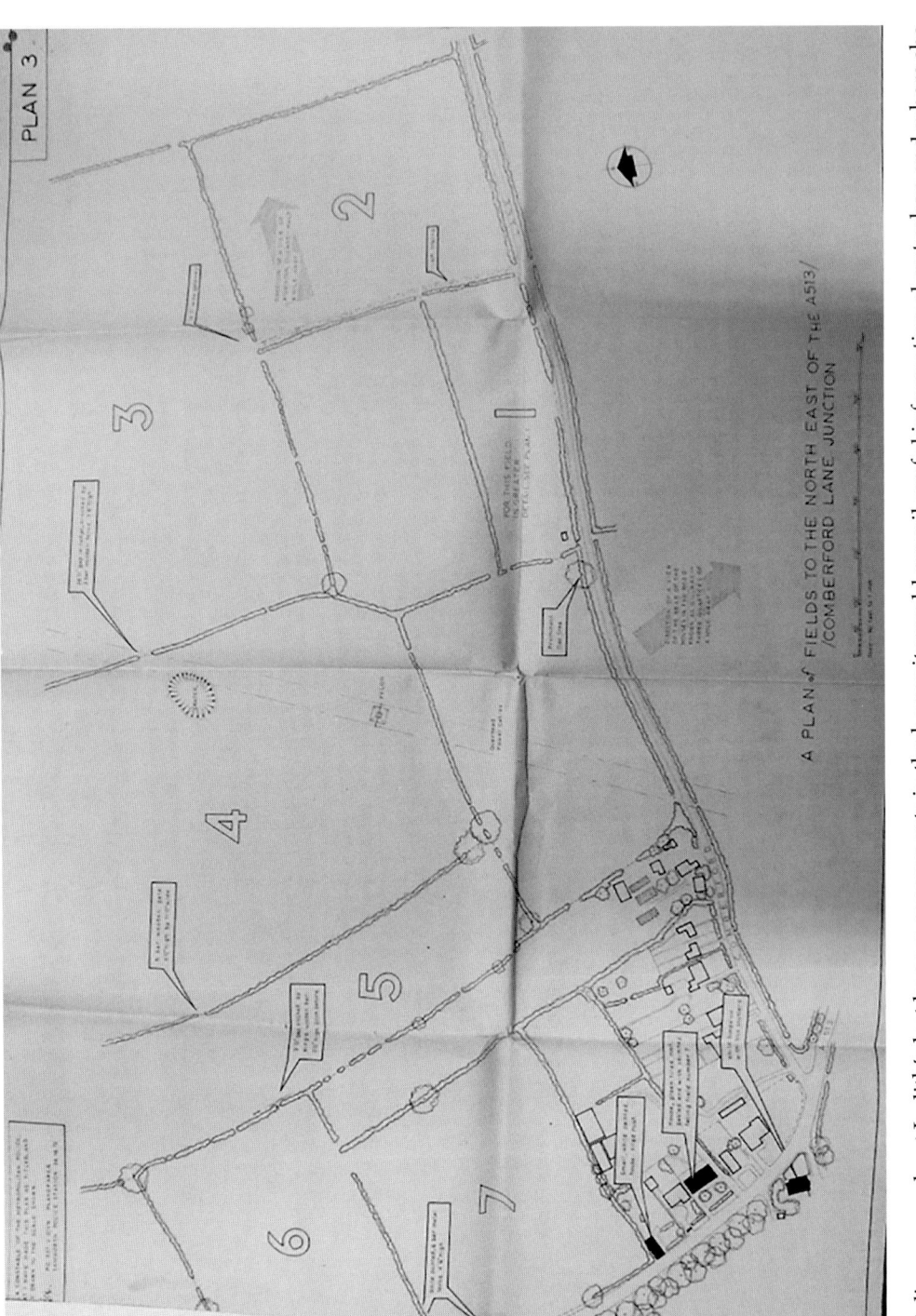

Police mapped out Judith's last known movements in the hopes it would unveil useful information about when and where she

The murder rocked the community of Tamworth and the effects were felt across the Midlands. (Mirrorpix)

Andrew Evans confessed to killing Judith, only to quickly recount his confession. However, a jury deemed him responsible for the murder and he was sentenced to life in prison. He served 25 years behind bars before his conviction was overturned. (Alamy)

Judith Roberts. (Unknown)

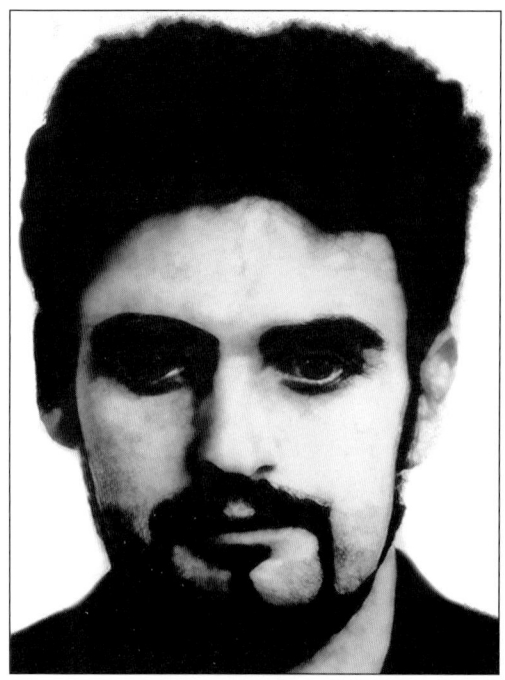

Left: Peter Sutcliffe booking photo for 1969 attack. (West Yorkshire Police)

Below left: Photofit likeness from the Wakefield attack, December 1972. (West Yorkshire Police)

Below right: Peter Sutcliffe booking photo after his 1981 arrest in Sheffield. (South Yorkshire Police)

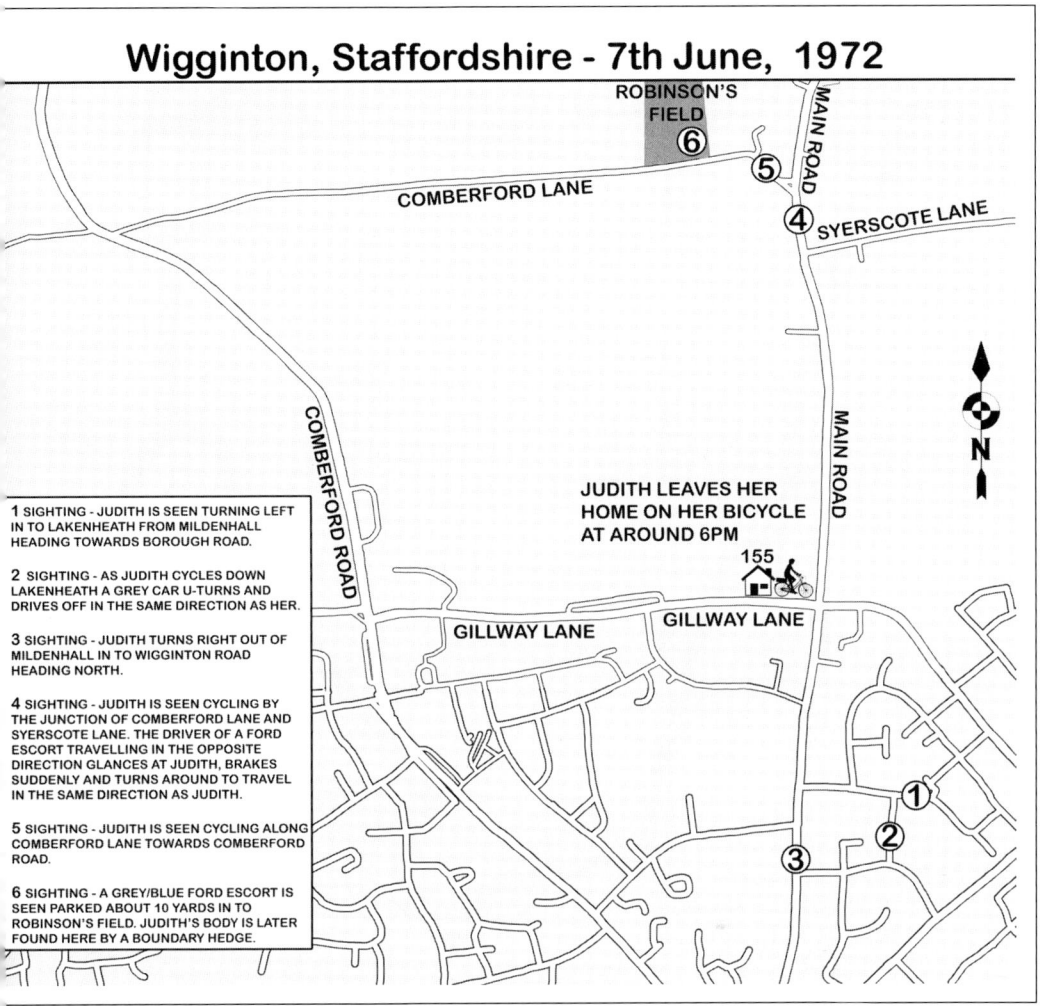

A map of Judith's cycle route, the last places she was seen alive, and the field (top right) where her body was found. (Chris Heath)

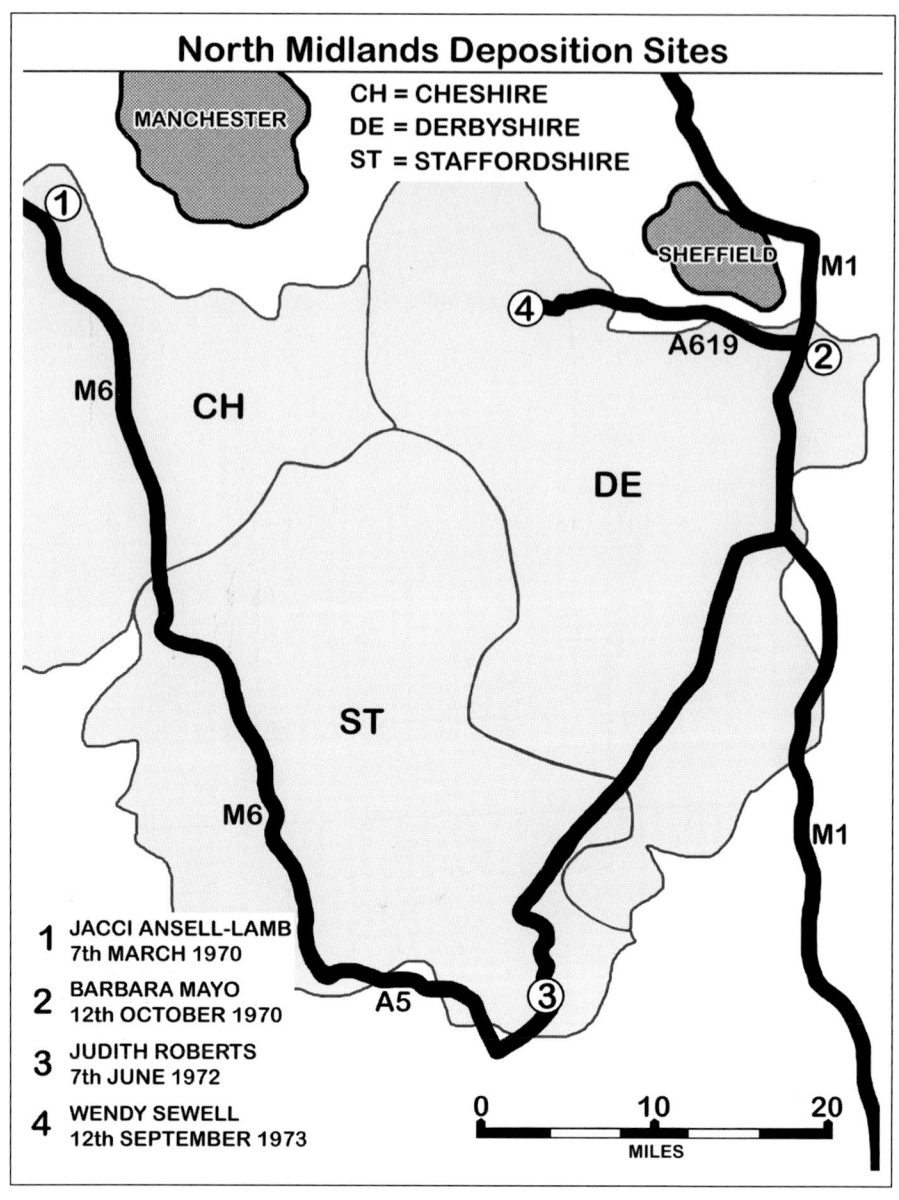

A map showing the locations of four similar crime scenes relating to the murders of Judith Roberts, Wendy Sewell, Jaqueline Ansell Lamb and Barbara Mayo. (Chris Heath)

The location of the fatal wound on Judith's head. (Chris Heath)

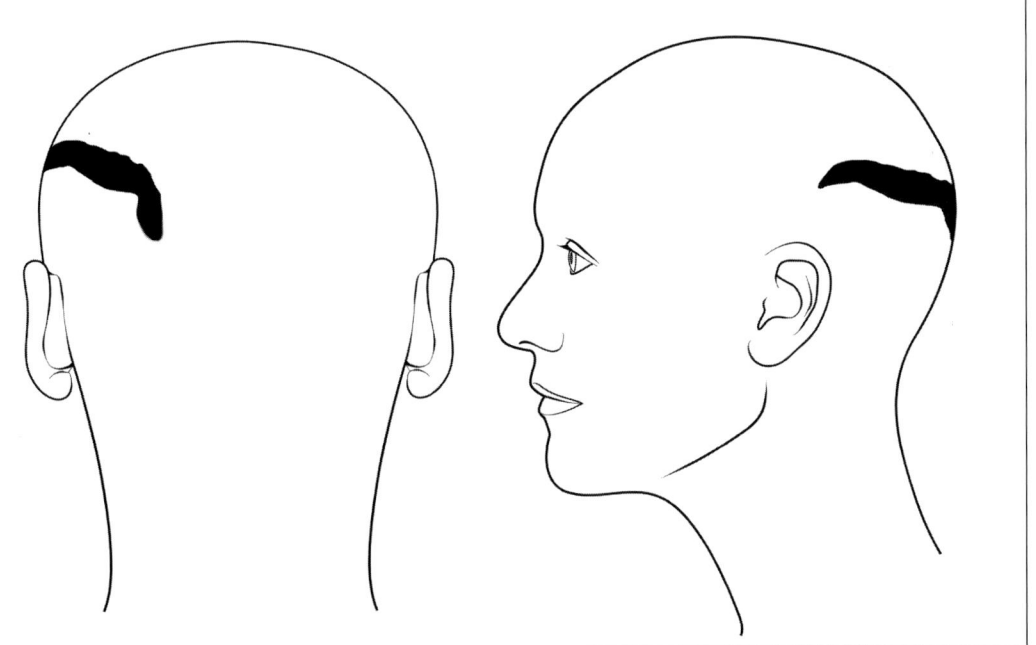

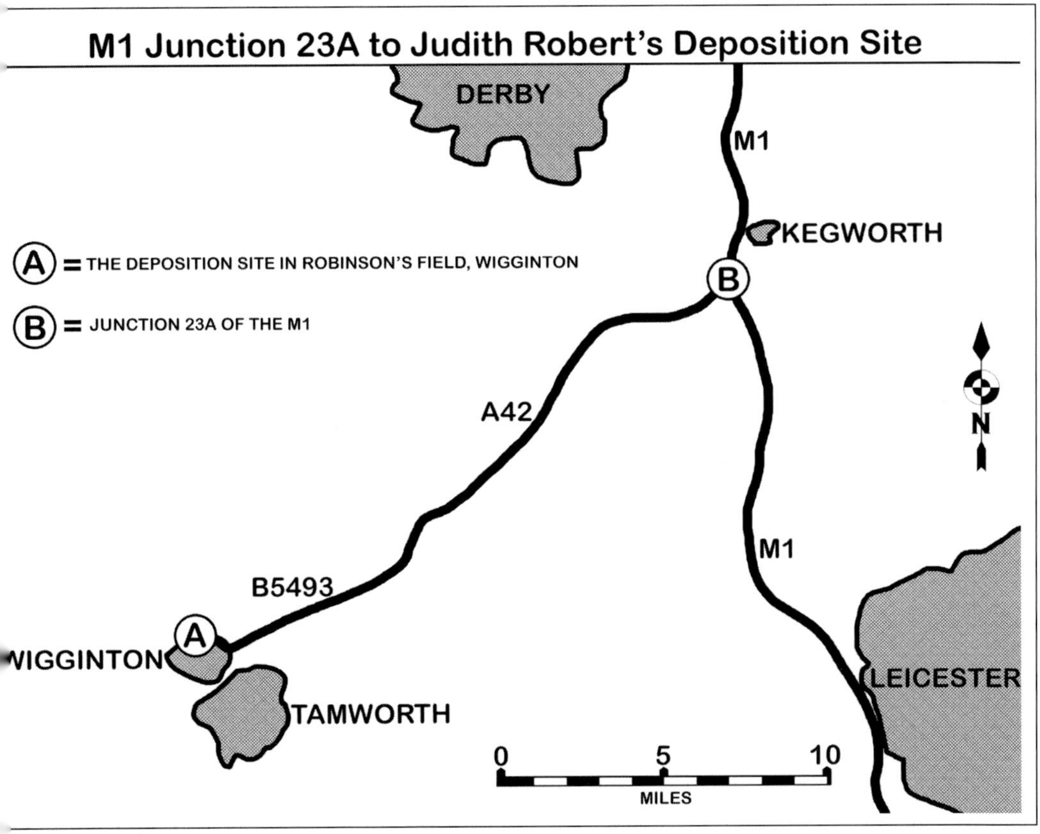

A map showing how close Judith's hometown was from the route Peter Sutcliffe would have likely taken down to London. (Chris Heath)

Above: After three days of searching for Judith, Staffordshire Police were called to a brutal scene in Robinson's field where the young girl's body had been hidden close to the perimeters of Cumberford Lane. (Unknown)

Left: A walling hammer – could this be type of weapon could have been used in the attack that killed Judith?

Andrew Evans showing police the location of Judith's body. (National Archives)

A pathologist quickly ruled that Judith had been murdered using a sheet of corregated asbestos however, during the early days of the investigation, police searched the hedges alongside the field where Judith's body was found looking for a murder weapon. (Mirrorpix)

I got a lift from there in a car to the end of the street where my Gran lives.'

DCI Wood: 'Since you were discharged have you ever been back to the Whittington or Tamworth area?'

Andrew Evans: 'No, I have never been to Tamworth. When I was at the Barracks I used to stay in most nights. If I did go out it was always to Lichfield.'

DC Colclough: 'How long were you in the Army?'

Andrew Evans: 'About eight weeks but I was in hospital at Cosford for a week just before I left the Army, but they couldn't do anything for me. About two days after getting back to the Barracks after leaving the hospital, they had me in the office and told me that I was being discharged because of my asthma.'

DCI Wood: 'Do you remember the date of your discharge from hospital?'

Andrew Evans: 'It was the second week of June, that was a Friday. I had a weekend pass and went to my mum's and reported back at Cosford on the Monday morning. That same morning I was taken by ambulance to Whittington Barracks. I remember that it was the next day, Tuesday, when they told me I was being discharged.'

DC Colclough: 'If you were in hospital what clothes did you wear when you were given a weekend pass?'

Andrew Evans: 'I'd only got my day uniform and I went home in that, because the next weekend I went to my Gran's on another weekend pass in my civvies.'

DCI Wood: 'If you left Cosford Hospital on Friday 2 June, and were discharged from the Army on 8 June, how could you have had a second weekend leave when you went to your grandmother's? If what you are saying is correct you were not in the Army'

Andrew Evans: 'All I know is that I had the weekend from Cosford, messed about at the Barracks all that next week, and then went to my Gran's the next weekend.'

DCI Wood: 'There seems to be a discrepancy about your date of discharge. Further enquiries will have to be made about this and other matters and I am going to take you to Tamworth. I then cautioned him.'

Andrew Evans: 'I suppose you've got to make sure it was me, it must have been me. Can you let my Gran know? I told her last night after the Detectives had been that I thought I'd killed her.'

DCI Wood at this point is depriving Evans of his liberty. He should have been told that he was either under arrest, or assisting with police enquiries and free to go at any time. Additionally, by this point Evans had been in police custody for some considerable time and should have been cautioned far earlier (as soon as they reasonably suspected that he had committed an offence). Particularly after having interrogated him for over an hour before taking him from Longton Police Station to the murder incident room at Tamworth.

***

Judges' Rules 1964
The Judges' Rules introduced on 27 January 1964, some eight years previously, are as follows:

Rule 1
When a police officer is trying to discover whether, or by whom, an offence has been committed they are entitled to question any person, whether suspected or not, from whom he thinks that useful information may be obtained. This is so whether or not the person in question had been taken into custody so long as they have not been charged with the offence or informed that he may be prosecuted for it. With the first rule it is still an enquiry and a police officer can ask questions without administering a caution. Indeed, no time limit is laid down as to how long he can continue questioning a suspect.

Rule 2
As soon as a police officer has evidence that would afford reasonable grounds for suspecting that a person has committed an offence, they shall caution that person or cause them to be cautioned before putting to then any questions, or further questions, relating to that offence. The caution shall be in the following terms:

> You are not obliged to say anything unless you wish to do so but what you say may be put into writing and given in evidence.

Judges' Rule 2 provides that as soon as an officer has evidence that would afford reasonable grounds to suspect that that person has committed an offence they must caution them; but the officer can still continue their questioning. When, after being cautioned a person is being questioned, or elects to make a statement, a record shall be kept of the time and place at which any such questioning or statement began and ended and of the persons present.

To clarify Judges' Rules 2 further, persons in custody should not be questioned without the usual caution being first administered. What does 'in custody' mean? This was decided in a legal case to mean 'in the custody of the police.' But what if the suspect is asked to go to the police station for questioning? Are they in custody? This again was decided by case law; that if a suspect was in a position to refuse to go the police station, they were not in custody and therefore did not have to be cautioned. On the other hand, when a person was interrogated in a room at the police station for three quarters of an hour and the police admitted, at the trial, that if they had tried to leave they would have prevented them, it was held that they were in custody.

Therefore, in Evans' case, once he was being interviewed by a senior CID officer at Longton Police Station he effectively became a suspect in Judith Roberts' murder and should have been told that he was under arrest and cautioned.

An interview is a structured conversation where one participant asks questions, and the other provides answers. The word 'interview' refers to a one-on-one conversation between an interviewer and an interviewee. However, what Evans received was an interrogation, a process of asking a lot of questions for a long time in order to get information.

Comfort and Refreshment
Reasonable arrangements should be made for the comfort and refreshment of the persons being questioned. Whenever practicable both the person being questioned or making a statement and the officers asking the questions or taking the statement should be seated.

Interrogation of Children and Young Persons
As far as practicable, children and young persons (whether suspected of crime or not) should only be interviewed in the presence of a parent or guardian, or, in their absence, some person who is not a police officer and is of the same sex as the child or young person.

Telephone Calls
A person in custody should be allowed to speak on the telephone to his solicitor or to his friends provided that no hindrance is reasonably likely to be caused to the processes of investigation, or the administration of justice by their doing so.

Rights
Persons in custody should not only be informed orally of the rights and facilities available to them, but in addition notices describing them should be displayed at convenient and conspicuous places at police stations and the attention of persons in custody should be drawn to these notices.

***

The interview continued:

> DCI Wood: 'On arrival at Tamworth at 6.25pm that evening he was seen by Detective Sergeant Williamson.'

> DS Williamson: 'At 6.26pm Monday 9th October, 1972, I was on duty in the Murder Incident Room at Tamworth when as the result of something said to me by Detective Chief Inspector wood, I went into the corridor where I saw the accused. He was sitting on a chair with his head in his hands. I said to him "What's wrong Andy? What are you doing here?"'

By this time Evans had been interviewed by no less than seven officers. No caution was given by DS Williamson, nor was Evans told that he was under arrest or free to go.

> Andrew Evans: 'After you left last night I told my Gran that I may have killed this girl.'

> DS Williamson: 'Why would you say a thing like that? Have you killed her?'

> Andrew Evans: 'I think so. I must have done because I can see a picture of her. I can see her lying near to a hedge. I can see her brown hair and she has got a mark across her face.'

> DS Williamson: 'What do you mean by that? Is it a bruise or blood or maybe a wound?'

> Andrew Evans: 'I think it's a wound and blood.'

> DS Williamson: 'If you have a picture of the girl have you got a picture of the man who is killing her?'

> Andrew Evans: 'A small youth about 5'4" with dark hair.'

> DS Williamson: 'Can you describe the instrument the small youth is using to kill the girl?'

> Andrew Evans: 'No, I can't see that but there is something lying across her right arm.'

> DS Williamson: 'What do you mean by that?'

Andrew Evans: 'I don't know. I can see something over her right arm as she is lying on her back.'

This is the first big discrepancy, as Judith Roberts was left face down.

DS Williamson: 'I was then joined by Detective Constable Peach who took Evans to an upstairs room.'

Evans has still at no point been told that he is under arrest or free to go.

DC Peach: '"Come upstairs Andrew." We went upstairs to a room in the building and Evans sat down by a table. He put his hands on the table and then placed his hands on the top. He appeared to be distressed.'

DC Peach: 'What's the matter Andrew?'

Andrew Evans: 'I keep seeing this girl. I can't get any sleep.'

DC Peach: 'What do you mean? You keep seeing a girl?'

Andrew Evans: 'I keep seeing her face.'

DC Peach: 'What else can you see?'

Andrew Evans: 'I can see her lying down.'

DC Peach: 'What else can you see?'

Andrew Evans: 'It's all confused. Have you got an aspirin?'

DC Peach: 'I'm afraid I haven't. Have you got a headache?'

Andrew Evans: 'Yes.'

DC Peach: 'He then put his head onto the table again. What are these tablets for? Indicating to two bottles which Evans had brought into the room with him.'

Andrew Evans: 'Them [sic] are for when I have asthma on and them go in there. He indicated to an inhaler.'

DC Peach: 'Are they any good to you?'

Andrew Evans: 'No.'

DC Peach: 'He then put his head on his hands. He did not say anything for a few minutes.'

Andrew Evans: 'After I saw you I was thinking if I killed her or not. I keep seeing her.'

DC Peach: 'I cautioned him and said [to Andrew Evans] "What can you see?"'

Once again Evans is not told if he is under arrest or free to leave.

Andrew Evans: 'This field.'

DC Peach: 'What sort of field?'

Andrew Evans: 'I'll show you. Have you got a bit of paper?'

DC Peach: 'I then gave him a piece of paper and he [Andrew Evans] said "I've got a pen." He then started to draw on the paper. (Labelled KP 3).'

The image drawn by Andrew Evans portrays [the] victim face up at deposition site.

DC Peach: 'He made comments during the time he was making the drawing. The Comments, Questions and Replies that I asked him are as follows:'

> Comment [DC Peach]: "That's the hedge sort of running like that."
>
> Question [DC Peach]: "What else?"
>
> Comment [DC Peach]: "There's a tree somewhere here."
>
> Comment [DC Peach]: "The girl's lying her be the hedge."
>
> Comment [DC Peach]: "There's something lying across her like this."
>
> Question [DC Peach]: "What is it?"
>
> Reply [Andrew Evans]: "I don't know. Something dark."
>
> Question [DC Peach]: "What does the girl look like?"
>
> Reply [Andrew Evans]: "She's young and got dark hair. I think it's long. Something like this."

> Question [DC Peach]: "Can you remember anything else? He made no reply."
>
> Question [DC Peach]: "If you remember anything else, carry on."

He did not say anything for about 3 minutes, then:

> Comment [DC Peach]: "I can see her shoes. They're something like this. They're blunt. Sort of round at the front."
>
> Question [DC Peach]: "What colour?"
>
> Reply [Andrew Evans]: "Dark colour."

He then paused for about 1 minute.

> Comment [DC Peach]: "There's the dress."
>
> Question [DC Peach]: "What about that?"
>
> Reply [Andrew Evans]: 'It's sort of ripped up the front like this.'
>
> Question [DC Peach]: "What colour?"
>
> Reply [Andrew Evans]: "It's white I think. It's got sort of flowers or petals on it."
>
> Question [DC Peach]: "Anything else?"
>
> Comment [DC Peach]: "There's a house. Black and white."

After this he [Andrew Evans] paused for about two minutes.

> Comment [DC Peach]: "There's something across her face."
>
> Question [DC Peach]: "What's that?"
>
> Reply [Andrew Evans]: "It's a mark, a scar or something. Like this. It could be blood."
>
> Question [DC Peach]: "Can you see anything else?"
>
> Reply [Andrew Evans]: "There's a road somewhere. I don't know where. Somewhere like this."
>
> Comment [DC Peach]: "I can see a bike. It's against this fence like this."
>
> Questions [DC Peach]: "What's it like?"
>
> Reply [Andrew Evans]: "It's fairly new."
>
> Questions [DC Peach]: "What colour?"
>
> Reply [Andrew Evans]: "Blue I think."
>
> Comment [DC Peach]: "The field's all rough."
>
> Questions [DC Peach]: "What do you mean by rough?"
>
> Reply [Andrew Evans]: "Sort of ploughed up and grassy.'"

DC Peach: 'At this stage DCI Stewart entered the room and I said to him: "This young man says he doesn't know if he killed the girl or not. He has drawn this sketch of a picture he says he can see."'

DCI Stewart: 'Is this true?'

Andrew Evans: 'Yes, but it's a bit confused.'

DCI Stewart: 'What do you remember?'

Andrew Evans: 'I remember her struggling and I grabbed her.'

DCI Stewart: 'By the neck?'

Andrew Evans: 'No, by the arm.'

DCI Stewart then left the room and DS Williamson came into the room.

DS Williamson: 'A few minutes later I went into the upstairs room where I saw Evans and DC Peach.'

DS Williamson: 'What's [it] that you've done?'

Andrew Evans: 'A picture of what I can see. How the girl is lying and things near to her.'

DS Williamson: 'I saw that Evans was looking rather pale. I said to him 'Are you alright?'

Andrew Evans: 'I'm hungry.'

By this time Andrew Evans, having been both in Longton Police Station and Tamworth Police Station, had been in police custody, and under more or less constant interrogation, although not told that he was under arrest, for some three-and-a-half hours, without so much as a drink of water.

> DS Williamson: 'I can fix you up with a couple of sausage sandwiches will that do?'
>
> Andrew Evans: 'Yes thank you.'
>
> DC Peach: 'Evans did not say anything for the next fifteen minutes. He just sat at the table with his head in his hands. [Detective] Sergeant Williamson returned to the room with sandwiches and I left the room. Approximately ten minutes later I accompanied Evans and [Detective] Sergeant Williamson to Tamworth Police Office.'
>
> DS Williamson: 'I returned sometime later and handed the sandwiches to him. After he had eaten them I took him to Tamworth Police Office where he was searched and placed in the cells.

At no stage from arriving at Longton Police Station at 3.00 pm until this point sometime after 7.00 pm on Monday, 9 October 1972 was Andrew Evans told that he was under arrest. So, there is a strong case here for unlawful imprisonment. During this time, he was cautioned by DCI Wood around 4.30 pm at Longton Police Station and around 6.30 pm by DC Peach at Tamworth incident room.

While on remand in prison, Evans wrote down his recollections for the defence, this is his continuing recollection:

I believe that the CID from Tamworth arrived and they began to question me. I remember being asked if I masturbated and told them that I did. I remember crying a lot and being given a sheet of paper on which to wipe my nose. I remember being asked why I did it, and I said that I didn't know. My head was splitting and I kept asking them for my asthma tablets. My tablets were at home and they kept saying they were going to get them, but they never turned up. I think that I was taken in a police car from Longton. I remember stopping at my Grans [*sic*]. The police went in and got my tablets and some tissues and told her that I was being held for questioning. I was then taken over to Tamworth. I can't remember exactly what happened when I got to Tamworth. But I remember being in the cells at Tamworth. Every time I was questioned I was taken out of the cells and into an upstairs room ... I remember a lot of interviews and a lot of questions thrown at me. There used to be two at a time questioning me. I didn't even have time to drink a cup of tea. If two went out then another two used to come in. I remember crying a lot. They asked me what they were going to do with me. I said that if I had done it, then I must be mad and I must need some treatment of some sort. When I was in my cells on the Tuesday, I asked for some paper and pencil so that I could do some drawing. I drew some airplanes. The Police told me that if I thought of anything I should write it down. I told them that I remembered a ploughed field with green growing over it and a low hedge about 3 or 4 feet high. I didn't say anything about a tree at this time. This was before I started doing any drawings. The first thing that I drew was the airplanes. I had not been out with the police to the scene of the murder at this stage. I drew the hedge and the rough ground. I did not draw the road in. I don't think I said anything to them about the white railings and those did not appear on my drawing. I don't think that I put any houses on my first drawing either.

DCI Wood: 'At 10.50am the following morning. Tuesday 10 October 1972, I saw Evans in the cells with DC Peter Colclough. As we walked into the cells Evans said "I've not slept very well. I can't get it out of my mind. Has anyone seen my mum yet?"'

DCI Wood: 'We are sending someone over to see her this morning, what is her address in Burton-on-Trent?'

Andrew Evans: 'She lives at 52 Bear Hill Road, Winshill. I wonder what she will do about it.'

DCI Wood: 'Don't worry about that at this time. Try and remember what you can and I will come and see you later.'

DCI Wood: 'At 11.30am with DC Colclough I saw Evans again and said, "Have you remembered anything else about it?"'

Andrew Evans: 'I remember dragging her off her bike. I was in a field and saw her riding along the road towards me, I just grabbed her by the arm and shoulder, pulled her off then we were just rolling about on the ground in the field. It was a very rough field.'

DCI Wood: 'Is there any more you can remember?'

Andrew Evans: 'It was rough. I don't know what [it] is was but it was uneven. I keep remembering bits about it.'

DC Colclough: 'What was the cycle like and can you remember what happened to it?'

Andrew Evans: 'It was just an ordinary bike, and I think I may have put it in the hedge.'

DCI Wood: 'If you think very carefully about it, it may come back to you. Try and remember and I will see you shortly.'

DCI Wood: 'At 12.15pm I saw Evans on my own [and said to Evans] "Are you remembering things more clearly?"'

Andrew Evans: 'I think I do now. I remember this field and struggling with her, there was a hedge and I could see this house. There were some other houses in the other direction in the distance.'

DCI Wood: 'Where was the house?'

Andrew Evans: 'There was this hedge here [indicated to his front] and the house was over there [indicated with his left arm at an angle to his left] I think I could draw the field and some of the things I remember. If I can have some paper I will write it down as I remember it.'

DCI Wood: 'I supplied with pen and paper and said [to Evans] "Anything you record may subsequently be used in evidence; do you understand?"'

Andrew Evans: 'Yes but I want to remember. I'm sure I killed her. Do you think I did it?'

DCI Wood: 'I can't answer that at this stage. Try to remember what happened on that day. I will come to see you later, but if you want anything in the meantime just ask to see me.'

DCI Wood: 'At 3.20pm the same day I again saw Evans at his request, and as I walked into his cell he said "I know now. I killed her."'

DCI Wood: 'Why do you say that? Do you recall what happened?'

Andrew Evans: 'I know I did it. I've put it down.'

DCI Wood: 'He then handed me three sheets of paper (marked SRW 1) containing writing and sketches, all three sheets were written on both sides, and I later numbered them 1–6.'

DCI Wood: 'Have you written this?'

Andrew Evans: 'Yes, that's how I remember it. I dragged her off the bike and we were rolling about in the field. I remember she was on her back and I was crouching over her. I had my hands on her shoulders holding her down and she started screaming and shouting. I remember picking something up that was nearby. It was round, I think it was a piece of wood and I couldn't get my fingers right round it, but I could hold it enough to hit her with it.'

(Indicating striking movement with his right hand.)

DCI Wood: 'What happened after you it her?'

Andrew Evans: 'She went quiet. There was a big bruise on her cheek.'

(Indicated by touching is left cheek below the eye).

Andrew Evans: 'I remember dragging her into the hedge, I pulled her by one arm and one leg, not both legs or both arms. I remember hitting her again then, but I don't know what I hit her with. There was something lying across her body on the right side. I don't know what it was, I've drawn it.'

(Indicated sketch on page 3.)

DCI Wood: 'Is the shape you've drawn as you remember it?'

Andrew Evans: 'Yes it was like that at the end, pointed. It was bigger than that though. It went further across her.'

(He then added the additional lines indicating the object extended across the body.)

Andrew Evans: 'There was a white fence. I walked across some fields and came to these white railings on a corner. There was a house nearby partly covered by trees and a lot of trees past the white railings. I climbed over the railings and went by the trees.'

(He then drew sketch of the white railings on page 3.)

DCI Wood: 'What is this?'

(Indicating sketch at bottom of page 2.)

Andrew Evans: 'I just drew it. That's how she looked.'

DCI Wood: 'What is this word?'

(Indicating Crageren on page 2.)

Andrew Evans: 'It's cardigan. That's what I have drawn. It was something like a cardigan, dark colour. I remember a van like a Post Office van. Not yellow, it was green. I think it was after I climbed over the railings. It stopped and I got in.'

DCI Wood: 'Where did you travel to in this van?'

Andrew Evans: 'I don't know. There was a man driving it. I think he was wearing something light coloured.'

DCI Wood: 'Was this before or after you had seen the girl?'

Andrew Evans: 'I think it was after. I think it was near the white railings.'

(Then drew sketch of van on page 4.)

DCI Wood: 'Is what you have written on this paper the truth?'

Andrew Evans: 'Yes.'

DCI Wood: 'Do you remember anything else?'

Andrew Evans: 'I remember now about the body.'

DCI Wood: 'What do you remember?'

Andrew Evans: 'All her legs were bare and white. I don't think I had intercourse with her. No I didn't.'

DCI Wood: 'Where were you when you saw her legs like that?'

Andrew Evans: 'She was on her back in the field and I was crouching over her holding her down with my hands on her shoulders.'

DCI Wood: 'What about her clothing? Do you remember?'

Andrew Evans: 'Her underclothes were off. I'd taken them off when she was unconscious. It must have been.'

DCI Wood: 'Why do you say that?'

Andrew Evans: 'I didn't have any bruises or anything when I got back to the barracks. If she hadn't been unconscious I must have had bruises.'

DCI Wood: 'You mean because you were not injured in any way she must have been unconscious when you removed her underclothing?'

Andrew Evans: 'Yes.'

(Pause.)

Andrew Evans: 'I seem to remember that she took them off herself. It was either that or she was unconscious.'

DCI Wood: 'What did you do with this clothing?'

Andrew Evans: 'I put it under the hedge.'

DCI Wood: 'What about the rest of her clothing?'

Andrew Evans: 'It was only her underclothing. Nothing else was off.'

DCI Wood: 'You say you dragged the body into the hedge. When did you do this?'

Andrew Evans: 'We rolled about in the field. Then I hit her once when she started shouting. She went quiet then. It was after when I dragged her into the hedge.'

DCI Wood: 'Why did you drag her into the hedge?'

Andrew Evans: 'To hide her I suppose.'

DCI Wood: 'Why did you want to hide her?'

Andrew Evans: 'I don't know, it was something I had to do. I don't know why I did it.'

Extracts from statement by DCS Harold Wright head of Staffordshire CID:

DCS Wright: 'At 8:50am on Wednesday 11th October 1972 together with Detective Chief Superintendent Saunders of New Scotland Yard, I saw the accused Andrew James Evans in an upstairs office at Tamworth Police Station. I then recorded notes of an interview which was conducted by Mr Saunders with the accused.'

We do not propose to include DCS Wright's full statement, simply because it is repetitive to the police interviews already conducted but to itemise the contents of his statement thus we have outlined the details of the statement:

Introduction of officers to Evans.

Evans was fully cautioned and caution explained in simple terms.

Evans then outlined his activities of 7 June 1972.

Evans was questioned at length over the previous police interviews.

Evans was then taken on a tour of the murder scene and the Whittington-Tamworth area as outlined further on.

DCI Wood: 'I later handed exhibit SRW 1 to Detective Chief Superintendent Saunders. On Wednesday 11th October 1972 I was the driver of the Police motor vehicle with other Police officers when Evans was taken round the Whittington, Elford and Comberford areas. On Thursday 12th October 1972 at 11:10am in company with Detective Sergeant Reeder I again took Evans around the same area. I was again the driver on this occasion. Whilst in Comberford Lane in the vicinity of where the murder had taken place, I was alone in the vehicle with Evans when he said.'

Andrew Evans: 'I keep wondering why I did it.'

DCI Wood: 'Well why did you do it?'

Andrew Evans: 'It must have been vengeance.'

DCI Wood: 'Vengeance against whom?'

Andrew Evans: 'I don't know. It was the army. They said they would find me a job when I left, and I had to see the R.S.M. about it. He kept saying "don't worry about it you'll be alright". I thought I'd be alright, but they let me down. When I came out they had done nothing for me.'

DCI Wood: 'If your grievance was against the Army why did you take it out on the girl?'

Andrew Evans: 'I don't know. I had nothing against her.'

Interview completed.

Andrew Evans' defence statement:

After that, I was taken out by the Police. The first time they took me out was on the Tuesday, I think. They took me straight from Tamworth to the place where the murder happened. I think I may have shown a road on my plan before we went out this first time, but I definitely didn't show the white railings until after we had been out. They took me into the field and said 'Do you remember anything about this field?' I said that they were not the right hedges. They were about 8 feet high, whereas the ones I remembered were only 3 or 4 feet high, and I could see over the ones that I remember and they were also very neat. They walked me up the side of the hedge. There were some plastic bags lying on the ground, and they asked me if I remembered anything, but the bags didn't mean anything to me. They pointed out some gaps in the hedge and asked whether those jogged my memory at all, but they didn't mean anything to me. They told me to have a good look round and asked me to let them know if there was anything that reminded me of anything. I looked around, but I didn't see anything that was recognisable at all. They then took me back. We drove straight on down Comberford Lane and I think I remember a fork in the road with a telephone box on it. I can't remember the time of the day but it was still light. I don't remember being questioned again that day, when I got back to Tamworth.

I did some more drawings. I sat down and had a good think about it. I showed the road on my drawings definitely, but I don't think I showed the white railings. I didn't show the tree on my drawings either. I did do the drawings of the house in the distance. I remember drawing something which had been straight ahead and to the left of me, as I stood with my right-hand side against the hedge looking along it.

I was again taken back to Lichfield for the night and brought back to Tamworth the following morning. I was questioned again. Then they took me out. This time we went to the Barracks. We went down the Barracks Road. We didn't stop at the Barracks, but we went down into the village. We stopped at the crossroads and they asked me if I remembered anything about the crossroads and whether it brought anything back. I said that I remembered driving round it. They then carried on. I remember on the way they asked me if I remembered anything else, but I said I hadn't. I didn't see anything further. I remember saying as we were going along the field was on the left-hand side of the road. I can't remember where we were when I said that but we had been going straight along the road for some time not taking any turns.

They took me into the field and asked me if I recognised anything then. I said I didn't. An old lady cycled by on her bicycle. I said I thought I remembered the girl coming down the lane from the same end that I had come in. I said that she would have been going past the hedge. I said that I had her under my arm and dragged her across the field to the other side.

We then walked back up out of the field onto the road and then back up a track which led to the side of the field. When we got a little way up, we stopped and the policeman said, 'Now which way would you go from here Andrew?' I looked around and saw a gap in the hedge straight ahead and said I thought I had gone through there. We could not walk straight across the field because it was a corn field, so we then went through that gap and into a field where there were some cows. He, [the police officer] was terrified of the cows but we went through the field and eventually we came out of the field by the white railings. I think that from then on we re-traced our steps but went back the way that they took us through the gap that I had originally pointed out in the second field. I know that when we had finished getting through the first route, he said that this didn't seem to be the right way. I can't remember why.

Based on Evans' statement, there is a very strong suggestion of the police putting false memories into his mind and, later, fabrication of evidence and of 'staging' the alleged route from Whittington Barracks to the crime scene and back. Evans continues:

When I got back I think I did some more drawings. I included the white railings this time. I drew the position of the body as

I remembered it and I drew the tree. I also drew a picture of the girl's face showing bruises and marks.

DCI Wood: 'At 3:15pm on Thursday, 12th October 1972, I was present at an identification parade at Tamworth Police Station. Evans, at his own request, position number 5 in a line consisting of nine persons, all of whom were dressed in Army uniform. As the witness Mrs Dorothy Milner viewed the parade I saw the accused Evans blush as the witness approached him.'

We argue that nothing can be or should have been inferred as to any guilt from this reaction. Blushing is the involuntary reddening of the face, usually triggered by emotions such as shyness, embarrassment or stress. Other areas of the body – such as the neck, ears and upper chest – can also be affected. As well as causing redness, blushing can sometimes make the affected area feel hot. What causes blushing? 'Normal' blushing occurs when a strong emotional trigger stimulates the nervous system, resulting in the widening of the blood vessels in the face. 'Abnormal' (severe or frequent) blushing can have both psychological and physical causes, including:

1. Social anxiety disorder (social phobia) – a persistent and excessive fear of social situations.

2. Generalised anxiety disorder – a long-term condition that causes anxiety about a wide range of situations and issues.

Andrew Evans: 'On the following morning I was put in Army uniform and had to go on an identification parade in Tamworth. I understand that I was not identified. It was a lady that came to go on the identification parade.'

The identification of an offender is a key aspect of any criminal conviction. This identification may be done by the victim of the crime and/or witnesses if there are any available. If someone can be identified as the offender, this will be one of the first pieces of evidence used in a criminal trial, with both the victim and any witnesses required to repeat the identification in front of the court. The traditional method of identifying an offender was to use a police identity parade. This involved the suspect being required to line up alongside others of similar height and appearance, with either the victim or a witness able to view the line-up. This would enable the victim or the witness to identify the offender by sight.

During a police identity parade, it would usually be the case that the police were aware of who the suspect was, due to their investigations, and the identity parade would be used simply as confirmation that the suspect was in fact the offender. In these situations, the other members of the identity parade may be police officers or simply people the police have picked off the street.

Potential issues with traditional police identity parade include the problems of wasting police time in looking for suitable participants – it used to take an average of ten weeks to organise a traditional identity parade in some areas – the following were key problems when using a traditional identity parade:

1. Emotional issues for victims and witnesses.
2. Potential for police interference.

Evans continued:

> After that, I was taken out again by the Police. We went down past the back of the Barracks to the crossroads at Whittington. We stopped and took a photo there. They told me to stand and point to the right of the crossroads and then took a picture of

me. This was the last photograph that was taken. I was then taken back to Tamworth. When we got back they told me a bit later on in the day they told me they were going to charge me. I think this was in the afternoon. I remember that I had a conversation with the sergeant from [New] Scotland Yard. I was in a room alone with him and he asked me what they were going to do with me. I said that they had better charge me because otherwise I might get out and do it again because I'm not sure myself as to whether I've done it or not. I said that the only way to find out would be for me to be charged and go to court. I said I'd never sleep another night and otherwise not knowing whether I had done it or not.

DCI Wood: 'At 6:15pm on Thursday 12th October 1972 I was present with other officers at Tamworth Police Station when Evans was charged by Detective Chief Inspector Stewart as he now stands charged.

Evans was cautioned.

Andrew Evans: 'Yes, I did it.'

A statement from Evans' defence statement:

My parents were in the Station and I went to see them, and I said to my mother 'I've done it'. I said I didn't know why. I said that I couldn't see myself doing it because I was sick at the thought of hitting anybody. I told my mother that I felt sorry for the parents but that I couldn't feel anything for the girl. I am sorry for what happened but I feel sure that I have not done it.

Eventually, after three days of interviews, conducted without his parents, a suitable adult, solicitor, or doctor present, Evans confessed to the murder, a confession which he later retracted.

Shortly afterwards, Evans who was taking prescribed drugs for depression, experienced what psychiatrists later called 'false memory syndrome', which we believe was something of a clairvoyant visitation, where he dreamt that he had seen Judith and the murder committed upon her and thought, wrongly, that he had actually witnessed or committed it himself.

Charged with the murder of the young schoolgirl, police destroyed 15,000 fingerprints they had acquired as part of their investigation. As far as they were concerned, they had found the killer. Although Evans had made a confession to Judith's killing he later retracted his statement and, before the trial commenced, decided to plead not guilty.

Chapter Eight

The Trial

On the morning of Tuesday, 3 April 1973, at Birmingham Crown Court, a jury of six men and six women sat down to opening arguments in the Andrew Evans murder trial. Defending before the judge, Mr Justice Chichton, was Mr John Owen QC. Prosecuting was Mr Brian Gibbens QC, counsel for the Crown. Evans' defence solicitor, Mr Bernard Bunce, was also present.

The prosecution argued that Evans had confessed and thus was guilty. The court would hear Gibbens argue that many of the details given by Evans to the police had not been published by the press and therefore were details that only the real killer would know.

Meanwhile, the defence argued that although Evans had admitted to the murder, he had been experiencing hysterical amnesia and that now he was certain he had not killed Judith.

Gibbens set about describing the scene of the murder site where Judith's body had been found, and how the child's body was discovered under the sacks, and that when they were removed, Judith was lying face downwards, naked from the waist down, with her blue anorak pulled up over her head. Her shoes were found near her body and her underclothes were lying mostly underneath her body, but there had been no sexual assault.

Gibbens explained to the jury how the postmortem examination showed the girl must have been killed some time before 7.30 pm on 7 June 1972 and death was due to fracture of the back of the skull following further severe blows, particularly to the left side of her face, and there was no evidence of a struggle.

Addressing the jury, Owen said that there were two possibilities in this case: that his client had in fact done the crime, or that he had witnessed the crime and had been so traumatised by his inability to do anything to help the girl that this had led to the false confession. He said:

> He will tell you that he is quite satisfied that he did not murder this girl and one of the reasons is that he does not feel like a murderer.

Owen went on to tell the jury that his client had been shown photographs of both the victim and of the item thought to be the murder weapon, but that neither did anything to 'stimulate him in any way'. Evans was still handicapped by a lack of memory, said Owen, who added:

> I shall call evidence which I hope will satisfy you that it is possible for people to have this hysterical lack of memory.

Owen then referred to a confession made by Evans to the police in which he said that he must have killed Judith because he kept seeing her face. Owen said:

> You may think that is more consistent with someone trying to get inside a memory which does not exist and work it out in a positive way.

Owen also spoke of the fingerprint on Judith's bicycle that had not proven to be a match for Evans' fingerprint, nor any of Judith's family, or the other 14,000 fingerprints that had been collected. In fact, this fingerprint had never been traced.

On the second day of the trial, 4 April 1973, the Home Office pathologist who had assessed Judith's body after it was found, Dr van der Merwe, gave evidence. When the defence cross examined Dr van der Merwe's findings and the Crown's notion that the sheet of asbestos was the murder weapon, Dr van der Merwe agreed that although the asbestos was originally thought to be an unlikely candidate as the murder weapon, as the item was the only piece of evidence at the scene where Judith's body was found which had Judith's blood on it, that in the absence of anything else, he, the police and thus the prosecution had concluded that this piece of asbestos was indeed the murder weapon. As part of his cross examination, Owen challenged and rubbished this theory, concluding that it was doubtful whether the asbestos could have had the weight and strength to have inflicted the injuries on Judith's head. Dr van der Merwe conceded that if there was anything other than the sheet of asbestos used then the offender must have carried it away. He then brought to the court's attention that he found no indication from Judith's injuries to suggest that she had been dragged into the thorn hedge during her attack; a slight injury to Judith's arm could have been a result of a defensive movement but he was sure that there were no signs of a struggle.

The defence also instructed an expert pathologist to challenge Dr van der Merwe's findings and conclusions. His statement is reproduced in Appendix I. It is interesting when reading the statement at (1) to (4) in conjunction with our thoughts that Judith was attacked with a dry-stone walling hammer. A walling or mason's hammer has one large striking face and the other end is ground into a long tapered horizontal chisel end that is used for dressing stone. The approximate weight of this item is a little over a kilogram – certainly heavy enough to cause fatal injuries if wielded hard enough.

The Home Office pathologist also agreed that, had the sheet of asbestos been the murder weapon, as alleged, then it would show signs of fragmentation in the aftermath of the force used to wield it, but no fragments of the item had been found in Judith's injuries. Judith had severe bruising beneath her left eye, an injury that Dr van der Merwe said was delivered by a strong person. He also stated that despite Evans' asthma, his condition would not have prevented him from carrying out the attack.

We believe that the facial injuries are consistent with Judith's killer dragging her quickly by her arm face down from the roadside and into the field, out of sight of passersby – as seen in Wilma McCann's case some three years later. In Wilma's case, injuries consisting of bruises and abrasions to her face made it obvious to Professor Gee, the pathologist to Sutcliffe's confirmed victims, that she had been dragged along the ground by her legs into a hiding area after being struck on the back of the head.

The press kept a keen eye on the proceedings throughout. Page three of the *Daily Express* on 5 April 1973 read:

> A young soldier tried to forget that he murdered schoolgirl Judith Roberts. But her pretty face kept haunting him until he confessed to police, a court was told yesterday.

The article gave a play by play of the proceedings in which Gibbens told the court that after being shown Judith's photograph, the soldier sobbed:

> 'I can't sleep. I keep on seeing her face. I wonder if I have done it.' According to Mr. Gibbens, police decided to check discrepancies in Evans' statement but what followed was 'a remarkable series of interviews' in which a sobbing Evans told police: 'It's this girl who was murdered at Tamworth. I keep on seeing her face.'

> Mr. Gibbens told the jury: 'You may think that this young lad, having killed the girl, was trying to banish the memory from his mind. But it was coming back to him, perhaps reluctantly. Because he could not admit, even to himself, that he was guilty' Mr. Gibbens told the jury that when his mother Joan saw her son in a cell, he told her: 'Don't cry mum, I am not sorry for what I did, I have no feelings about it ... It's you I am sorry for.'

Also cross-examined were soldiers from the barracks where Evans had been stationed at the time of the murder. One recalled how Evans' asthma had acted up during a cross country run. He agreed that Evans' condition was what had led to him being relieved from the army and that Evans did not want to go and was upset about the decision. Another soldier, Private Peter Raymond Ogden, claimed that on 7 June 1972, he had gone off to play sports and had left Evans behind on light duty. In court he described how, when he returned later that afternoon at approximately 4.30 pm, that Evans was not there and instead, arrived back later that evening. When Ogden said that when he questioned Evans about his whereabouts, he received no answer. However, Owen pointed out that now, Ogden had given conflicting statements, having given and signed a statement in January 1973 to the defence solicitors that said he could not remember Evans going out on the day of the murder. He agreed that he could not really remember what happened that day.

The defence called Evans' mother to give evidence on the third day of the trial. On the stand, Joan Evans, from Burton-on-Trent, painted a picture of a placid child with a desire to be just like every other child his age. Mrs Evans explained that from the age of 4 her son had suffered from asthma and that this had led to him being discharged from the army after only a few weeks of him joining the unit. 'As a child he constantly wanted to do the same things as other children,' she said.

> I had to constantly tell him that he could not do this or that. If he tried to do these things he became wheezy and had to be given injections.

She told the court that her son had never been violent or aggressive. A written statement, submitted by Evans' grandmother, Irene, said that:

> Andrew used to look at the papers but only at the stars, the cartoons, and the picture of the dead girl.

She said that this had only started to happen after the police called at the house for a second time, approximately four months after Judith had been killed – until this point there is no evidence to show that Evans had mentioned Judith or made reference to her murder. DS Terence Reade of New Scotland Yard also took to the stand, where he described a visit to Evans' mother, stating she had discussed with him the fact that her son had killed Judith, telling her:

> If they had kept me in the Army, this might not have happened.
> I worked too hard and that is why I had an attack.

DCI Wood, who had been one of the officers to interview Evans in October 1972, agreed that Evans told them that the murder was an act of vengeance against the army.

In his evidence, given on the fourth day of the trial, DCS Wright was asked by the prosecution about Evans' attitude when he was interviewed by DCS Saunders and DCS Wright on 11 October 1972.

DCS Saunders described Evans as 'calm' and 'having answered questions in a considered way.' According to DCS Saunders:

> [Evans] would think about what he was asked and was giving answers with due consideration.

When prompted further he said:

> My impression was that he was given [giving] answers that were truthful and that he was giving us his recollection of events that had happened in June.

He was firm in his answer when he told the court:

> I never got the impression he was making it up at any time.

DCS Saunders was cross-examined by the defence about the amount of publicity that was given to Judith's case. There can be no doubt that DCS Saunders was a veteran police officer; a well-respected and meticulous detective. However, when discussing the press' coverage on Judith's murder, he said that, to the best of his knowledge, there were details left out of their reporting, such as the fact that Judith had been found face down and also details about her watch.

He told the court that his belief that Evans was the killer was solidified when Evans was asked to show police where the body had been found. DCS Saunders said that he had given Evans no indication as to where that might be, except for the fact that it was in the Tamworth area. He went on to say that the field was mentioned to the press but the exact spot where the body was found was not indicated. It is worth noting that DCS Saunders was the final witness to be called in the prosecution's argument, and to the jury, this detail alone might have sealed Evans' fate as a convicted murderer.

We can see that at least one newspaper article from a major publication had printed a map showing the location in which Judith's body was found within forty-eight hours of Private Barrie Keith Gibson stumbling upon the site – almost four months prior to Evans being questioned by police. The *Birmingham Evening Mail*, published on 12 June 1972, shows a police officer at the gate of Robinson's Field. A few feet from him, behind the privets that line the field, an 'X' marks the exact spot where Judith's body was found. The caption reads:

> The murder scene today. A cross marks the spot where Judith's body was found. Her home is arrowed in the distance.

In the exact same story, beneath a picture of Judith is a hand-drawn map showing the area and the adjoining roads that make up the route Judith last cycled; Wigginton Lane, Wigginton Road, Gillway Lane, Ashby Road and Comberford Road. Another 'X', placed most of the way along Wigginton Lane, is labelled 'body found here' and marks the murder scene. Owen was quick to refute DCS Saunders' claims. The trial was moved to a Birmingham television studio for an hour so that the jury could also watch the televised and highly reported reconstruction of Judith's final movements, which took place just weeks after her body was found and featured her twin sister Ann posing as Judith.

DCS Saunders also gave evidence about 'Mr X', a farmer's son in Tamworth, who had been considered a prime suspect for Judith's murder. The New Scotland Yard chief said that 'Mr X', who lived not far away from the murder spot, denied killing the girl, but it was true he had exhibited an aggressive attitude towards women in the past. DCS Saunders said that the man had given conflicting accounts of where he was on the day of the murder, and how this had arisen their suspicions, but that the enquiries into the man's movements were carried out 'in very great depth'. The chief officer described to the court how the man had frightened and followed women in the very lane along which Judith had cycled to her death. When asked by Owen about an incident in April 1972, in which the same suspect had admitted an offence involving children, DCS Saunders agreed that had been the case. Gibbens told the court that 'Mr X' was a red herring and that there was no justification for any suspicion of the farmer's son.

Evans himself gave evidence over two days (9 and 10 April 1973), explaining that on 7 June 1972 he went to the camp NAAFI at around 2.30 pm, had tea, and then at around 6.30 pm went back to the NAAFI, where he says he stayed watching television. He told the court he was confident he had not left the barracks that day and that when he was questioned by police about his whereabouts he truly did believe he had been in the company of the two men named in his statement but that he now realised that was wrong. When police told him the two men could not have been in his company, his thoughts began to spiral and that, as he had been proved wrong about one aspect of his memory, he began to fear he was wrong about others. It was during his time on the stand on 9 April 1973 that the jury were told of the truth serum tests that were done on Evans at his request. The defence counsel explained that despite the tests, the last of which was performed the previous weekend on Saturday, they had failed to jog Evans' memory about the day of the murder.

The main crux of the prosecution's arguments centered on the statement Evans had given to the police and signed, prior to his arrest, in which he had admitted to killing Judith. Evans did relay details of the death scene to police although he got the colour of the bicycle wrong and had originally referred to hitting Judith over the head with a piece of wood. However, the prosecution and pathologist had suggested the murder weapon was a piece of asbestos. He had also made reference to Judith wearing a dress with flowers on it, but papers had always described Judith's dress as 'checkered'. You will remember that during the police interviews, Evans even drew a picture of Judith with the murder weapon lying across her. Then, when police talked to him again, Evans had told them:

> I know now. I did kill her. I pulled the girl off the bike ... she started kicking and shouting. I remember picking something up and hitting her with it. She went quiet.

When discussing the investigation and police questioning, Evans said that after thrice being administered truth drugs at his behest, he remembered seeing a girl's legs in a field. The tests were carried out at his own request 'because I could not remember.' Describing the vivid images he said:

> The girl's legs were sticking up from her body. I am leaning up against a gate and looking into the field. On the other side, is a person standing up. Below him, and right against this person, there are a girl's legs sticking out. One leg is bridged and the other is straight out.

Evans went to the police the next day asking to see the photograph to see if the girl was the girl in his dreams. Evans agreed that he had told the police several times that he had killed her but could not remember the exact words that were used. Gibbens asked Evans:

> Are you trying to say that you don't remember anything now but you did at the time?

The defendant answered:

> I don't think I am trying to forget, but I can't remember.

Unsatisfied with the answer Gibbens commented:

> Either you were telling the truth at the time or this was a great work of fiction completely down to the smallest detail.

Reading from the statement, Gibbens highlighted a passage in which Evans described what he had done to Judith's body in the aftermath of the attack:

> I [Evans] put the clothes under the head before I hid the body. There was something lying across the body. It was like I said and like I have drawn.

Gibbens directed another question at Evans:

> What was lying across the body?

To which Evans replied:

> I don't remember.

Gibbens pressed further, asking how it was that he remembered during his interview that there was something lying across the body. Evans told him that although he remembered saying that to the officers, he could not remember now why he had made reference to the item 'lying across Judith's body'. Gibbens referred again to Evans' prior statement:

> She had a very big dark mark on her face where I struck her.

Gibbens asked Evans:

> Something must have made you very angry to have hit this girl like that. Was it true?

Evans told him:

> I was only trying to think at the time.

When the judge asked Evans what had prompted him to think that he had killed Judith, Evans told him:

> It was the logical assumption because I had these facts in my mind.

Evans told Gibbens that he deliberately tried to impress police by saying that he killed the girl. 'I don't know why,' he said. When asked to describe the 'mystery man' he saw in the field, Evans replied:

> It was a male. But I can tell it's not me.

Having read how this young man came to be embroiled in this major crime we are convinced that he, in his highly emotional state, experienced a vivid clairvoyant vision of Judith's murder and wrongly thought that he had actually witnessed or committed it himself. Asked by Owens:

> Is there anything that has been adduced in the evidence for the prosecution that he brought to your memory a feeling that you might have killed this girl?

Evans, firm in his reply, said:

> No, quite the contrary in fact. I know now that I have not done it.

Besides being on trial for murder, Evans' character was otherwise somewhat of an upstanding citizen, having been described by his previous headmaster of 'good character'. There can be no doubt that Evans was a vulnerable person and as such, psychological evaluations are and were paramount when it came to this case. Dr Anton Stephens, a consultant psychiatrist and deputy medical superintendent at Highcroft Hospital in Erdington, who saw Evans eight times between 1 December 1972 and 7 April 1973, gave evidence on 11 April 1973, the penultimate day of the eight-day trial. Dr Stephens told the court that it was his opinion that Evans was uncertain of anything that had happened on the day of the murder.

> He has a great facility to create fantasies in compensation for certain problems of his own. He then cannot distinguish between the fantasy he has made and the bedrock of fact on which it is made. He is in many ways a minor edition of the character called Walter Mitty.

Dr Stephens was making reference to American author James Thurber's short story *The Secret Life of Walter Mitty*, which is centered on an inept male daydreamer with PTSD who fantasises in order to escape the reality of his mundane job. Originally printed in *The New Yorker* in March 1939, the story developed into a cult favourite, and the term 'Walter Mitty' has been used to reference 'an ordinary, often ineffectual person who indulges in fantastic daydreams of personal triumphs.' When asked by Owen if it was possible for his client to have imagined his involvement in the murder without having been involved at all, Dr Stephens agreed that this was possible. Asked by Owen if, in his professional opinion, Evans had been suffering from amnesia when he was seen by police on 8 October 1972, Dr Stephens told the court:

My opinion is that he had no memory at the time of his personal involvement with the killing of Judith Roberts.

He also told the jury that the drugs given to Evans were only used as a way of allowing a man or woman to access repressed memories and bring them to the surface with less reluctance.

The following day the defence was reopened. Taking to the stand, Dr Reginald Washbrook, a medical officer of Winson Green Prison in Birmingham, described Evans as having a 'definite hysterical make-up'. Dr Washbrook told the jury:

> by hysterical I don't mean a person who yells at the top of his voice at the slightest provocation. I mean a person who tends to use his imagination a little more than the so-called average among us.

In a further explanation Dr Washbrook said that:

> All of us have an element of hysteria in our nature and he has a little more drama in his make-up.

Owen asked Dr Washbrook if it was possible that, while under the influence of the truth drug, that Evans had described a true picture of what he had seen or if he had been telling a lie and making it up. Dr Washbrook replied:

> I can say that it must have been a true picture of what was in his mind at the time.

He went on to explain that it was recognised in psychiatry that a man or woman giving an account of things that had happened would fill in the gaps of the memory in order to create a coherent picture. When the defence had rested, the prosecution took to scrutinising Dr Washbrook and Evans' changing recollections of the day of the murder.

> Was it your opinion yesterday morning that the fact that he was at the scene and not in the barracks would be remembered by him at the time he was giving evidence?

Gibbens asked the medical officer. Dr Washbrook simply replied: 'Yes.' The prosecution continued:

> Was it further your opinion that when in the witness box he said that he was not at the scene but was in the barracks, he was consciously changing his story?

To this Dr Washbrook said:

> When you put it to me that way, I have to say yes.

After proceedings came to a close on 12 April 1973, after eight trial days, the jury retired to consider the verdict. It took them a total of three-and-a-half hours to reach what was a unanimous verdict and on 13 April 1973, despite all the evidence given in defence of Evans, the jury accepted the confession and Evans was jailed for life. This was then changed to

> being detained during Her Majesty's pleasure.

A young Evans was to be sent to a young offenders' prison, where he would remain until he was 21 years old. From there, he would be sent to an adult jail. As he was led down, Evans simply thanked his solicitor. His mother, Joan, wept as her child, flanked by two guards, was removed from the dock and returned to the cells where he would remain until he was transferred to the detention centre where his life tariff would begin.

It is obvious from the proceedings that the investigation into Evans had been bungled, and although some might feel that Evans admitting to the crime is strange in the first place, it must be noted that apart from Evans' 'confession', no other evidence was presented. Despite the prosecution's arguments that Evans was the killer, they failed to present any scientific evidence against him, nor any eyewitnesses who could support the Crown's arguments.

It must also be remembered that false confessions are a known psychological reaction to a number of environmental factors. Evans' case was more than a decade before the Police and Criminal Evidence Act 1984, strict legislature which capped detention times for all suspects at a maximum of ninety-six hours, with court oversight after twenty-four hours, and a minimum eight hours rest within any twenty-four hour period. This meant that suspects were free from questioning or other investigation process, a window carved out for prayer and mealtimes. All interrogations were subject to mandatory recordings and the presence of a lawyer and medical assessment upon arrest where necessary. Prior to 1984, such rights were not given to suspects, including Evans. Even reading back over Evans' answers to the court, it is clear he is vulnerable, and his answers at times are confusing, which could have come across to a jury as him being evasive and misleading. Police were unaware of what had been reported in the media, and witnesses who could have accredited Evans with an alibi were unreliable (not necessarily through any fault of their own but just at the prospect of how much time had passed.) For sensitive and vulnerable youths, police questioning is a minefield and an overwhelming amount of pressure which, in the right context, can yield judicial results, but when mishandled, can have devastating consequences.

Chapter Nine

The Secret Years

It is our belief of us that the real culprit for this crime never stood trial for it. We theorise that Sutcliffe committed a mid-week murder when travelling to or from London to see his girlfriend Sonia, who at this point was in Bexley Psychiatric Hospital, while he was on holiday, and thus diverted from his normal method of operation by working night shifts. As we have heard, within weeks of the police cautioning him about the 'stone in the sock' incident, which was classed as an aggravated assault, Sutcliffe was arrested in possession of a hammer. He was later charged with going equipped for theft, instead of being in possession of an offensive weapon, and after appearing before magistrates, was fined £25. After losing his job at the cemetery for poor time keeping, Sutcliffe held a number of labouring positions, including working for the local water board digging up old pipework and making trenches where he would use pickaxes, spades, shovels and similar tools. A pickaxe handle was used some three years later in the murder of Wendy Sewell in Bakewell, Derbyshire. Around 1969 Sonia's influence transformed Sutcliffe's style from the late 1960s fashion of 'cowboy' dressing and his love of rock 'n' roll and country and western, to a more 'refined' style of music. They started going to see her sister Marianne give platform piano recitals in London and other venues, taking in the occasional opera and ballet. What address Marianne had at that time isn't clear, but she subsequently had three addresses in west London, including two in Alperton, situated close to the North Circular A406 and a link to the start of the M1 motorway at Hendon, and in all probability, this is where she had settled originally. This is very significant, as two murders that occurred during 1970 – that of Jacqueline 'Jacqui' Susan Ansell-Lamb in Mere, Cheshire and Barbara Janet Mayo in Ault Hucknall, Derbyshire – and one attempted murder – during April 1972 in St Albans, Hertfordshire, where Marie Burke was left for dead – were hitchhikers who all started their fateful journey north on the M1 at Hendon.

Jacqueline 'Jacqui' Susan Ansell-Lamb

Jacqui Ansell-Lamb had been born on 21 September 1951 in St Pancras, London, to parents Percy 'Jack' and Jean Ansell-Lamb. The marriage between Jack and Jean broke down and Jack remarried, this time to a woman named Peggy. During September 1969, Jack and Peggy moved from London to St Ives in Cambridgeshire with their son Jeremy, but Jacqui – who was an 18-year-old secretary – didn't want to leave London, so she stayed on with a friend, 20-year-old Judi Langrish, the two girls sharing a flat together. Jacqui was typically modern, and liked dancing and discos, and would not have fitted into the quiet Cambridgeshire scene.

During February 1970, Jacqui moved with Judi to the near comparable night scene of Manchester, where both shared a flat in Whalley Range. Jacqui got a permanent job as a secretary. Both had returned to London the following month, on 6 March 1970, in order to collect their remaining clothes, and decided to stay for a party at Earl's Court. There, Jacqui met 23-year-old David Sykes and they spent the Friday night, Saturday and Sunday morning together at his address in Blackheath Park. Jacqui had told Judi that she would catch a train to Manchester on the Sunday.

On the Sunday afternoon, 8 March 1970, David Sykes drove Jacqui the 15 miles to Hendon and the start of the M1 North for her to hitchhike to her flat in Whalley Range, Manchester. Jacqui didn't relish the idea of hitchhiking to Manchester, but neither of them had the train fare. He dropped her off at 2.30 pm. That was the last that was seen of her by anyone who knew her. The day Jacqui was due to return home came and went and, with no sign of her friend by Monday, Judi reported her flatmate missing.

The murder took place in Mere, near Knutsford, in neighbouring Cheshire, some 0.5 miles from the Chester to Manchester Road and some 70 miles north-west of Wigginton. Jacqui was last seen on 8 March 1970, hitchhiking in north London at the start of the M1. Although it was only March, the new decade started out a promising and exciting one for young females such as Jacqui. On 1 January 1970, the age of majority in England and Wales was reduced to 18 from 21 under the Family Law Reform Act 1969. That same month, on 22 January, the Boeing 747 touched down at Heathrow Airport, making it the first jumbo jet to have landed in Britain. As the month of March began, the first National Women's Liberation Conference was coming to a close at Ruskin College, Oxford, a motion that would see equalities for women in the United Kingdom established, including financial and legal independence for women.

By the time summer arrived, Jacqui would have been the first wave of teenagers able to vote in the general election. It was, without a doubt, an exciting time to be an 18-year-old woman in the United Kingdom. Tragically, Jacqui would never experience the opportunities afforded to her generation. On Saturday, 14 March 1970, a farmer came across her partially stripped body, lying spread-eagled, face down, in Square Wood off Bentleyhurst Lane. Jacqui's blue and white miniskirt and maroon shoes were lying beside her body. It was reported that she had been beaten about the back of the head, suffering blunt force trauma, and then strangled with an electrical flex. She had also been sexually assaulted. Bruises on her neck and cuts on her face indicated that she had bravely fought back against her attacker. On 2 February 2014, author Chris sent an

FOI request to Cheshire Constabulary regarding Jacqui's case. On 19 February 2014, they sent the following refusal:

Dear Mr Clark

I refer to your recent request for information under the Freedom of Information Act 2000, as set out below:

Please could you inform me whether an offender DNA profile has been obtained from the Jacqueline Ansell-Lamb murder of 9–14 March 1970. Were her injuries consistent with being struck on the back of the head and asphyxiation use of a rope ligature.

If so is there a DNA link to the Barbara Mayo murder of October 1970 in Derbyshire. Was Peter Sutcliffe's DNA profile obtained to test on your victim.

In accordance with section 1(1) (a) of the Act, our response is as follows:

The Cheshire Constabulary can neither confirm nor deny that it holds the information that you are requesting. To give a statement of the reasons why neither confirming nor denying is appropriate in this case would itself involve disclosure of exempt information, therefore under section 17(4), no explanation can be given. To the extent that section 30 (3) applies, the Cheshire Constabulary has determined that in all the circumstances of the case the public interest in maintaining the exclusion of the duty to neither confirm nor deny outweighs the public interest in confirming whether or not the information is held.

Public interest considerations in confirming or denying that the information is held. Whilst there maybe public interest in knowing whether or not the police have information that could potentially lead to the apprehension of the victim's killer. To confirm or deny the existence or otherwise of the information requested would also inform the killer. Whilst the public's curiosity may be satisfied, the killer knowledge would be greatly enhanced. There can be no public interest in confirming or denying information that would also aid the murderer of an 18-year-old girl.

If I can be any further assistance in this matter, please do not hesitate to contact me.

If you are not satisfied with the decision applied in this case I enclose for your attention a copy of the Constabulary's appeal procedures.

Regards

John Gannon
Information Compliance
Professional Standards Department

The killer had covered her body in her purple-coloured maxi-coat. It was a meagre attempt to conceal the horror of what had been done to her. The act of posing victims' bodies has been an instrumental characteristic of organised killers for centuries. While there are earlier examples of the terms 'serial murderer', the English term and concept are generally accepted to have been coined by the late FBI profiler Robert Ressler, who developed his works in the 1970s, when the special agent, and former army major, used the term 'serial homicide' in a 1974 lecture at the Police Staff Academy in Hampshire, England. The FBI describes a serial murder as a

> series of two or more murders, committed as separate events, usually, but not always, by one offender acting alone.

Dr Scott Bonn postulates that FBI agent and profiler Roy Hazelwood is responsible for the concept of organised and disorganised killers, a notion rooted in the study of thirty-six serial predators conducted by FBI agents John Douglas and Robert Ressler. Although such a term was defined by Ressler in the twentieth century, it was obviously not the first time such a person was thrust into the limelight in the aftermath of multiple slayings. A notable killer whose crimes reflect this term was the English serial killer 'Jack the Ripper', who terrorized Whitechapel, east London half a century before Ressler was even born. The still unidentified killer roamed the capital in 1888, targeting at least five women and placing their bodies in positions as a means of adding a shock factor to his crimes. The police and public were served up the ghoulish remnants of his depraved pastime every few weeks between August and November before he appears to have ceased activity indefinitely. The act of posing bodies is a very unique characteristic of an organised serial killer. Robert D. Keppel et al wrote in 2004 that the objective is

> to thwart an investigation, shock the finder and investigators of the crime scene, or give perverted pleasure to the killer.

Despite being of an age where Jacqui had the potential to belong to a wave of young women who had new freedoms and exciting opportunities, she came to belong to a group of people whose deaths were characterised by the likes of a truly disturbed individual. The posing of bodies by the 1970s and at the time of Jacqui's murder was nothing new, however efforts were now being made to use this act as a way of defining the type of killer who had struck as a means of identifying them. When it came to studying the behaviours of the attacker dubbed by the media as 'The Yorkshire Ripper', it was clear to psychologists that he fell into Ressler's category of an organised killer. Many of his victims were posed, their bodies left in grotesque fashion.

While Jacqui's murder remains officially unsolved, a huge question mark hangs over her case as to whether Sutcliffe could have come into contact with her.

During September 1970, Sutcliffe's future wife, Sonia Szurma, began her three-year teacher training in London at the Rachel McMillan College in Deptford, Greenwich, firstly doing painting but then turning to pottery after a few weeks of arriving there. Her father had insisted that when she was in London for the course she should live with her sister Marianne in west London. She was her only social contact during that time, apart from Sutcliffe. Sutcliffe's intentions were to visit Sonia there on weekends and holidays, when he would drive there as soon as he had finished work on a Friday in his Morris 1000.

Over the weekend he would sleep in the car, or in a tent pitched in the grounds of the college Sonia was training at. During the early hours of Monday, he would drive back from London, arriving home again in Bingley a few hours before he was due to clock in at the start of another week. This was a journey that had the option to take the A1 Road and link onto the M1, where our next victim was murdered a few months after Jacqui.

Barbara Mayo

Barbara Mayo, 24, six years older than Jacqui, and training to be a teacher, lived with her boyfriend at 40 Rockley Road, Shepherd's

Bush, west London. During the first week of October 1970, they were returning from a visit to County Durham to buy four new wheels for their car, which had broken down at Catterick in North Yorkshire. The couple had left the car at a local garage, and planned to travel back to pick it up once it was repaired. They hitched back to London via the A1/M1. On Monday, 12 October 1970, Barbara got up at about 7.30 am and left her home half an hour later in order to hitchhike to Catterick to collect the car. Her journey started by tube train to Hendon, where the M1 motorway begins on the journey north. Going on the premise that she would have quickly gained a lift on her ill-fated journey around 9.00 am, Barbara should have reached Junction 26 in Derbyshire, some 140 miles north, sometime between 11.00 and 11.30 am. However, she never made it to the garage, and nothing was heard from her after she left that morning. The following lunchtime, the day after she had left, the Catterick garage was contacted. They confirmed that she had never arrived to collect the repaired vehicle. She was reported missing, and a vast search of the motorways was undertaken to try and trace her by her boyfriend and a private detective. Another young woman, closely resembling Barbara, was seen in a White Morris Traveller Estate at around 4.00 pm, which was widely part of the police investigation.

Barbara was reported missing, and a vast search of the motorways was undertaken to try and trace her by her boyfriend and a private detective. Some six days after she was last seen standing on the side of the M1, on Sunday, 18 October 1970 Barbara was found dead. Like Jacqui, she was found face down. She was fully clothed, but with her clothing in disarray with her jacket spread over her body in a lonely wood approximately 20 yards down a track off Hodmire Lane, Glapwell near Ault Hucknall in neighbouring Derbyshire. The site was approximately 50 miles north-east of Wigginton. She had been strangled with a ligature and beaten about the head. The police declined to comment as to whether she had been subjected to a sexual assault.

This was another murder that had occurred the same year that Jacqui was killed, the details of which were almost identical, and the setting somewhat similar. Elements of the two murders mirrored one another; both women had been beaten about the head, killed by a blunt force trauma. The second, and almost identical circumstance, was that both had hitchhiked from the same point at the London end of the M1 motorway, and both were found in a very similar fashion, with their bodies being dumped in the vicinity of quiet country lanes. However, there are no DNA tests to confirm that the same person killed both women. If Sutcliffe was the person who murdered Jaqui, then in all likelihood he killed Barbara too. The cases remain unsolved.

Watching television footage from 1971, police officers from these two cases refer to the fact that both Jacqui Ansell-Lamb and Barbara Mayo had been brutally raped; however, there were no semen samples. We suggest that they were not penile-raped but, as in Josephine Whitaker's case, with the giant rusty Phillips screwdriver. On the night of Josephine's death, Peter Sutcliffe had been out drinking with long-time friend and drinking partner, Trevor Birdsall. Shortly after closing time, Sutcliffe dropped Birdsall off and drove towards Halifax in his grey Sunbeam Rapier. As Sutcliffe got to Savile Park he spotted Josephine Whitaker, who was walking alone. He quickly parked up, tucked a hammer and giant rusty Phillips screwdriver into his pocket, and began to follow her. A few minutes later Sutcliffe caught up with Josephine and asked her if she had far to go; she mentioned her trip to her grandmother's house, and that it was quite a walk home. As they made progress across the field, in a section without lighting, Sutcliffe hit Josephine from behind with his ball pein hammer and knocked her to the ground. Sutcliffe noticed people coming along the pavement, so dragged the dying Josephine 30 feet into the darkness, away from the road. Josephine was moaning loudly when Sutcliffe pulled her clothing back, turned her over, and stabbed her twenty-one times with his screwdriver in her chest and stomach, and six times in the right leg. He also thrust the screwdriver into her vagina, over and over again. Josephine's body was discovered the next morning; her skull had been fractured from ear to ear. Examiners also found size 7 Wellington boot prints near the corpse. Both Jacqui's and Barbara's murders were linked at an early stage in the Cheshire Police and Derbyshire Police investigations and, as we understand it, following progresses in DNA during 1997 the police were able to find a sample on Barbara's clothing; a fingerprint on the clothes she was wearing at the time of her murder. This opens up several possibilities:

1. Barbara's attacker left the DNA sample on her clothing.
2. An accomplice left the DNA sample on her clothing.
3. The item of clothing was second-hand, and the DNA sample had been there when Barbara acquired it.
4. That Barbara had had a liaison with someone at some stage in the past prior to being in a relationship.

The fingerprint has never been identified. Crime scene procedures in 1970 were very poor, and the fingerprint could have been innocently transferred to the clothing either prior to Barbara acquiring the clothing, or from officers undressing the body, bagging the clothes, placing them in storage, or from some other innocent source. In our opinion, the fingerprint and DNA do not necessarily belong to the murderer and cannot therefore be used to eliminate Sutcliffe. To confirm this, a former police officer has very recently contacted Chris and said:

> Agreed, and what is amazing is that the clothing had been dry cleaned so I, a Policewoman, could wear it for the reconstruction. I was part of the 1997 enquiry, and we were led to believe they had a straightforward DNA sample. So you're telling me something new here. Even working on it for six months.

Going deeper into this element, Chris has obtained a copy of the original Associated Television reconstruction footage of Barbara's journey. This reconstruction was broadcast on television a week after the motorway checkpoints were set up, covering Barbara Mayo's last known movements from her home in Hammersmith to the M1 and from London to Derbyshire, using a female model. The footage starts with

> Reg Harcourt report to camera from the police incident room in Chesterfield.

We then see a reconstruction of events leading up to Barbara Mayo's death.

We see a woman dressed in the same clothes as Barbara. In a BBC *Crimewatch* programme from 1991, there is further vintage footage showing the reconstruction, and a loudspeaker announcement states:

> The girl you can see is wearing the actual clothing of Barbara Mayo, who was murdered a short distance from the 29 intersection of the M1 motorway on Monday the twelve of October 1970.

So clearly, in the years between the murder and the 1997 'breakthrough', numerous people handled Barbara's clothing – including the wearer in the reconstruction – rendering the fingerprint and subsequent DNA useless, and in all probability not connected to Barbara's killer.

During the autumn and winter of 1970 Sutcliffe continued to drive back and forth along the M1 from Bingley to London to visit Sonia. This went on for a few months and then, during spring 1971, Sutcliffe installed himself in a bedsit near to Sonia, and was able to survive on what he earned from doing bits of motor mechanic maintenance and joinery. He had taken his toolbox in the car with him, and in his tools of trade he would have access to numerous items that could be made into weapons, including hammers, saws and screwdrivers – the very kind of weapons he amassed for the later murders and attempted murder series of 1975 to 1981. From September 1970 until autumn 1971, Sutcliffe was preoccupied with Sonia being in London. Much of the time he was left mainly to his own devices, either living in London or travelling back and forth along the M1 between the capital and West Yorkshire. At his 1981 trial, he told James Armstrong Chadwin, for the defence, that he worked nights because he didn't like the 'mission' he claimed he had been chosen for. When asked by Mr Justice Boreham whether, during his time in London, Sutcliffe was able to resist the 'messages' telling him to kill, he replied simply: 'I didn't see any prostitutes.'

During 1971 Sutcliffe was seeing a 15-year-old girl, with their affair going unchallenged for the next three years. She later said:

> He'd make love to me in every imaginable way... but we never had straight penetrative sex, he didn't like it; it used to disturb him even talking about it.

The lady in question remarked that she was still a virgin at the end of the affair. What's more, in Gordon Burn's book *Somebody's Husband, Somebody's Son*, it is reported that Sutcliffe confessed to his friend sometime in the 1960s that he had been caught with a 'girl' from his estate and that he had once taken a fifth former to Arnsdale for the weekend. While there is no strict time frame mentioned on when this occurred, it does appear to have been some time in the 1960s, during/after Sutcliffe's job as a gravedigger in Bingley cemetery and likely before he met Sonia Szurma in 1967. If this time frame is correct then Sutcliffe would have been in his early 20s, and the fifth-form girl between the ages of 15 and 16. He met Sonia when she was 16 years old and he was 21 years old.

During the authors' extensive research, Chris Clark was contacted by numerous women who claimed that they encountered Sutcliffe in their early teens, some as young as 13 years old. Two women in particular, named in Chris' book *Inside The Mind Of The Yorkshire Ripper* as 'Child A' and 'Child B', claimed that they encountered Sutcliffe in Fulham in London in the late 1970s when they were just 13 and 14 years old. Sutcliffe offered them a lift to Sunderland, which they accepted, but were freaked out by Sutcliffe's behaviour and, once in Sunderland, quickly vacated his cab and reported the strange encounter to Northumbria Police.

Similarly, another woman reached out to claim she was followed by a man she believes to be Sutcliffe in Leicestershire in 1980. This woman, who was 15 at the time, alleges she was walking home from school at around 3:40pm when a man in a lorry drove alongside her and asked her the time. She answered him, not wanting to be impolite, but his attention then turned to her, and he enquired if she was 'free'. To which she replied 'no', and fled up her street, Belgrave Avenue, and ducked into her home. She saw the man walk the length of her street before doubling back and leaving. The incident left her shaken. The woman claims after Sutcliffe's arrest the following year that she recognised the man in the arrest photo as the man who had followed her that day. She was too scared to come forward for fear of what her association with the man who claimed he only killed sex workers might mean. There have been a lot of similar claims that have come to fruition since Sutcliffe's arrest and death. The true tally of his attempts to pick up and attack young women remains unknown but ever in question.

When Sonia went back to college for her second term during September 1971, Sutcliffe told her that he would travel down to see her as regularly as possible; and in fact, he stayed there for a few weeks to keep her company. During November 1971, Sutcliffe worked at Baird Television's factory on the packaging line. This would continue until April 1973, when he left after being asked to go on the road as a salesman. After the Easter holiday of 1972, Sonia continued her teacher training course in London, with Sutcliffe continuing to travel back and forth to see her when the opportunity arose. Could he be behind the following attack?

Marie Burke

Marie was seen thumbing a lift at the beginning of the M1 at Hendon, in a similar fashion to that of Jacqui Ansell-Lamb and Barbara Mayo, during 1970 at around 6.30 pm on Tuesday, 18 April 1972. Later, at 8.00 pm, she was seen thumbing a lift outside the White Horse public house at Leverstock Green near Hemel Hempstead, heading to St Albans. Half an hour later, as darkness was falling, an off-duty policeman travelling along the A4147 Hemel Hempstead Road on the outskirts of St Albans saw a pair of bright pink trousers some 30 yards off the road in a lorry drivers' layby – just 1 mile from where Marie was last seen. Upon investigation, the officer found her unconscious body covered with her own imitation fur coat – this ultimately saved her life. The attack upon her was described as 'particularly savage' by the detective chief superintendent and SIO. Marie had extensive serious head injuries, and she had been left for dead. The placing of the coat over the body after the attack is significant, as this was how both Jacqui Ansell-Lamb and Barbara Mayo were found. It later became a feature of Sutcliffe's attacks on Irene Richardson in February 1977, Vera Millward in May 1978 and Josephine Whitaker in April 1979.

Marie was rushed to the Mount Vernon Hospital in St Albans; she remained in a coma for nearly three weeks before starting to recover. A retired Hertfordshire detective who was on this case tells us that Marie suffered brain damage to the extent that she was never able to remember who picked her up from outside the pub in

Leverstock Green, but her injuries are consistent with being hit on the back of the head with a hammer. Another retired officer, who was aide to CID at the time, recalled how horrific the assault was considered at the time, and that Marie was psychologically scarred and later admitted to Hill End Psychiatric Hospital on more than one occasion. She was also seen wandering around St Albans from time to time.

Author Chris was informed by another retired Hertfordshire officer that, some five years after the attack – during 1977 – he had received a telephone call from Marie Burke to see if any further progress had been made into her attack. He sadly had to inform her that there hadn't been. She made a further call during the following years.

During May 1972, Sonia suffered a nervous breakdown and was admitted to Bexley Hospital in London. She eventually returned to Bradford as a voluntary outpatient and Sutcliffe helped her with what was to be a slow recovery that would continue up until May 1976. Whilst still working at Baird Television, Sutcliffe visited her most weekends and holidays during 1972 up to that July. At his 1981 Trial, Sutcliffe said to the judge, Mr Justice Boreham:

> It was while I was there (Baird Television) that I got a telegram from Sonia saying, 'Meet me at King's Cross Station'. That was all, no time, no date, nothing. I thought there was something strange about it. As I had seen her in London a week before when she was highly excited and agitated and had lost a stone in weight and her face was ashen grey. So I took it to her parents. She was still their responsibility. Her father dashed off to London and found she had had a nervous breakdown and had been taken to Bexley (a psychiatric hospital).

During this time, Sutcliffe continued to visit her and she eventually returned to Bradford, becoming an outpatient at Lynfield Mount Hospital. As previously mentioned, from May 1972 onwards Sonia was in a psychiatric ward in Bexley, London and Peter Sutcliffe would make infrequent trips from his night shift work at Baird Television to see her, when she did eventually return home, she was in and out of circulation depending on her nervous disposition and he was left to his own devices much of that time.

Chapter Ten

The Appeal

Andrew Evans had spent the best part of fifteen years behind bars before his first appeal was lodged. At the end of his eight-day trial he was convicted of Judith's murder and sentenced to life imprisonment. Advised he had no grounds for an appeal, Evans accepted the status quo.

But in 1994, his case came to the attention of the media, following a chance encounter with a member of Greenpeace while Evans was an inmate at HMP The Verne in Dorset. Steve Elsworth went to the jail to give a talk and, after meeting Evans, he later returned to interview him. While Evans relayed his story, Elsworth took detailed notes of the case, which he passed on to John McLeod and Allister Craddock, two producers at Carlton Television. The case was subsequently featured that year on Central Television's regional magazine programme in the Midlands presented by John Stalker, *Crime Stalker*, and later in 1997 on a documentary, *The Nightmare*.

Evans also wrote to the human rights organisation Justice about his case in 1994, and they agreed to take it up. Evans was represented by their solicitor Kate Akester, winning the right to appeal against his conviction. In the 1997 documentary, Akester explained how there were strong grounds for believing the conviction unsafe. Evans was not eligible for parole unless he admitted he had killed Judith, but he had long abandoned his guilty verdict and was still vocal that he had not been the one to murder her.

Evans' hearing took place at the Court of Appeal in December 1997 before three formidable judges: Lord Chief Justice Lord Bingham,

Mr Justice Jowitt and Mr Justice Douglas Brown. Lord Bingham, who lived to be 76 before he succumbed to lung cancer in 2010, was described as 'the greatest English judge since the Second World War'. Mr Justice Jowitt was knighted for his work in 1988 and oversaw the trial of the 2001 murderers of Ross Parker who was stabbed, beaten with a hammer, and repeatedly kicked, by a gang of British Pakistani men in a racially motivated attack. Evans was represented there by Patrick O'Connor QC, while the Crown was represented by Bruce Houlder QC.

The appeal documentation, dated 3 December 1997, was addressed to The Lord Chief Lord Bingham of Cornhill. It read as follows:

> [that the appellant] Andrew James Evans appeals (with an extension of time to apply for leave and leave to appeal granted at the outset of the hearing) against his conviction of murder by a jury in the Crown Court at Birmingham on 13 April 1973.

The document, which is a public record, outlined the facts of the case as follows:

> Judith Roberts was a 14-year-old schoolgirl who was murdered in the early evening of 7 June 1972 in or near a field north of Tamworth in Staffordshire. She left her home to ride her bicycle around the lanes nearby. Her body was discovered 3 days later under a pile of hedge clippings and plastic fertiliser bags close to the hedge inside Robinson's field. Her bicycle lay in the hedge close to her body. When found, she was lying face downwards and the bottom half of her body was unclothed. There was no sign of sexual penetration. There were nineteen separate wounds on the girl's head, including one major blow on the back of her head which fractured her skull and caused brain injury from which she died. The medical evidence

indicated that this was the first blow, probably struck when she was standing upright, and it would have rendered her unconscious immediately. The discovery of the body provoked an intensive police investigation, with much publicity locally and nationally.

The appellant was on 7 June 1972 a private soldier serving in Whittington Barracks, just outside Lichfield and four or five miles away from Robinson's field [sic]. He had had an unsuccessful childhood and adolescence, suffering from low self-esteem and a sense of failure. He had joined the army in April 1972 in the hope of making a successful career and proving himself. His service career had however been interrupted by an attack of asthma, to which he was prone, and by which he was afflicted during a training run. The decision had been taken that he should be discharged from the army on medical grounds. This reinforced his sense of failure. He was discharged from the army and handed in his uniform on 8 June 1972. He then went to his parents' home, but his relationship with them was not good, and he moved on to stay with his grandmother.

On 27 July 1972 the appellant attended at the police station at Longton, Stoke-on-Trent to fill in a proforma issued to all soldiers who had recently been discharged from Whittington Barracks. The proforma invited him to disclose where he had been between 6pm and 10.30pm on Wednesday 7 June 1972 and he replied:

> 'In barracks and never left on this date. Was discharged the next day on medical grounds suffering with asthma'.

He named three fellow soldiers in the barracks who could verify that he had been in the barracks between those hours on that day.

After his discharge from the army and while living with his grandmother the appellant worked as a salesman but was depressed at his low earnings and remained disappointed at leaving the army. On 29 September 1972 he consulted his general practitioner complaining of depression, and Valium was prescribed. The appellant showed no interest in or concern about the murder of Judith Roberts. On the evening of Sunday 8 October 1972 police officers called at the grandmother's house to ask the appellant further questions about the proforma he had filled in. They had discovered, and put to the appellant, that two of the soldiers he had named had left the barracks before 7 June [1972], and they had been unable to trace the third soldier. They further suggested that the appellant had been wrong in giving 8 June as the date of his discharge from the army, putting it to him (wrongly) that he had left the army a week later, on 15 June. The appellant became agitated and 'very shaky' to the extent that one officer asked the appellant if he was all right. His grandmother explained that he suffered with his nerves when he was spoken to and became excited, which brought on his asthma. The appellant took a tablet and appeared to calm down. He made a written statement confirming that on 7 June 1972 he had been in the barracks all day. He expressed inability to remember exactly who had been with him. Before the officers left he asked them what would happen to anyone who committed a murder like that, and one of the officers replied that such a person would be in considerable trouble but would need his head examined. After the officers left, the appellant became 'really worked up' and said to his grandmother that it might have been he who committed the murder. She reassured him but she could see he was 'very worried'.

On the following morning, 9 October [1972], the appellant told his grandmother that he was going to the police station because he wanted to see a photograph of the murdered girl. He was obviously worried, as if the matter had been on his mind all night, and she was unable to reassure him. At about three o'clock that afternoon the appellant called at the Longton police station. He was seen by a police cadet who noticed that his body was shaking and he was stuttering when speaking. In answer to questions the appellant said that he wanted to see a picture of the girl in the Tamworth murder. He added that he was very nervous and kept dreaming about the girl. The cadet took him to see a Detective Sergeant. He was still nervous and shaking and, according to a statement made by the Detective Sergeant,

> 'The boy Evans rushed a couple of paces forward to a desk next to mine and placed both hands, outstretched on the desk and started crying and sobbing, heavily and loudly. It was impossible to converse with him. I obtained a chair and placed it underneath him and said, "Sit down son, calm yourself". Evans sat down on the chair. He was still crying. He was leaning forward with his head between his knees and his hands on his face. He continued crying and he was left alone to calm down.'

Asked by the Detective Sergeant what he wanted, the appellant repeated that he wanted to see a photograph of the murdered girl, adding

> 'I was in the Army; I don't remember where I was'.

The Detective Sergeant and a Detective Inspector who was also present then took the appellant to see a Detective Inspector, who, after a few formal questions, asked the appellant why he was so upset. He replied:

> 'It is this girl who was murdered at Tamworth. I keep seeing a face. I want to see a picture of her. I keep seeing her face. I wonder if I've done it.'

He was asked to describe the face, and gave some details, adding a description (not an accurate description) of the dress which the girl had been wearing. He gave her age as about fourteen. He asked the Detective Inspector why he kept seeing this face. The Detective Inspector asked whether the appellant thought he had 'done it' to which the appellant responded by clenching his fists at each side of his head and saying

> 'I don't know whether I've done it or not ...'

He was asked if he had ever been to Tamworth and replied

> 'I don't know. I could have done. I forget where I've been. I can go down streets and in houses and later I wonder how I got there.'

Asked about his movements after he had been discharged from the Army, he gave some details about his visit to his mother and went on:

> 'You see, I can't remember. This is how I am. I could have got home the next day. I don't know where I've been. That is why I keep wondering if it's me that's done this murder. Can you show me a picture to see if I've ever met her?'

The Detective Inspector asked him if he had done the murder and he replied:

> 'This is it. I don't know. Show me a picture and I'll tell you if I've ever seen her.'

The interview ended at about 3.30pm, and throughout the appellant had been crying more or less continually with short periods when he had become more composed.

At about 4.15 pm on the same day the appellant was visited in the police station by a Detective Chief Inspector and a Detective Constable. The appellant repeated his request to see a photograph of the murdered girl, adding that he thought he had killed her. He was told to calm himself and then to say why he thought he had killed the girl to which he replied:

> 'I keep seeing her face all the time. I can't sleep. I've got to know if I did it because I think I must have done.'

He was still in a very distressed state. During the interview the appellant began to cry bitterly, slumped forward in his seat, and became so distressed that it was necessary to help him to another room in the police station to allow him to recover. He was in distress due to his asthma, and several times repeated

> 'I must have killed her.'

At the end of this interview the Detective Chief Inspector cautioned the appellant for the first time. He replied:

> 'I suppose you've got to make sure it was me, it must have been me.'

The appellant was taken to the police station in Tamworth and sat in the corridor outside the murder incident room where he was seen by a Detective Sergeant, one of the officers who had visited the appellant the evening before. The appellant was sitting on a chair with his head in his hands. Asked if he had killed the victim he replied:

> 'I think so. I must have done because I can see a picture of her. I can see her lying near to a hedge. I can see her brown hair and she has got a mark across her face.'

Asked about the mark across her face he replied that he thought it was a wound and blood. The officer asked him whether he had a picture of the man who was killing the girl and he described a small youth about five foot, four inches with dark hair. He was taken to another room in the police station by another officer, who described him as distressed, putting his hands on the table and then putting his head on top of the table. He repeated that he did not know if he had killed the victim or not but kept seeing her. He was then cautioned. He was asked a series of factual questions to which he gave answers, some of them later shown to be accurate and some inaccurate. He made a drawing which he gave to the officer. Towards the end of the interview he sat in silence for (according to the officer) fifteen minutes. He was sitting at the table with his head in his hands.

The appellant's drawing bore no obvious resemblance to Robinson's field [sic] and showed the victim lying on her back. At 11.30am on the next day, 10 October 1972, the appellant was interviewed again. He was not cautioned. In the course of his answers he described how he had dragged the victim off her bike, grabbing her by the arm and shoulder and pulling her off. He then said that they had rolled on the ground in the field, which he described as very rough. He said that it was just an ordinary bicycle and

'I think that I may have put it in the hedge'.

He was interviewed again at 12.15pm on the same day, and again no caution was administered. He added some further details. He then asked for a pen and paper with which he was supplied, being warned that anything he recorded might subsequently be used in evidence. He said that he understood that but wanted to remember. He added

'I am sure I killed her. Do you think I did it?'

The officer declined to answer but asked him to try to remember what happened on that date.

Visited at 3.20 pm the same day, the appellant told an officer that he now knew that he had killed the girl. He said:

'I know I did it. I've put it down.'

He supplied the officer with three sheets of paper, both sides of which he had covered with writing and sketches. He described a struggle with the victim during which she had been lying on her back and he had been crouching over her and gave some details of the locality. He described a green van in which he had been given a lift to or from the scene and described the victim's legs as 'bare and white'. He said:

'She was on her back in the field and I was crouching over her holding her down with my hands on her shoulders'.

He thought that he must have taken her underclothes off when she was unconscious, because he had no bruises when he got back to the barracks. He spoke of putting the underclothes under the hedge, and dragging the body into the hedge. The appellant's written narrative confirms much of what he said in his oral answers. His sketches are not easy to decipher, and in certain respects (as, for example, in his indication where the fight between him and the victim had occurred) appear to be very wrong.

Late that night, at about eleven o'clock that evening, the appellant was visited in the cells at Tamworth and he handed an officer four sheets of paper, covered with drawings and writing on both sides of each sheet. He was then taken to Lichfield police station where he was closely questioned about what he had drawn and written. No caution was administered. He gave a description of the weapon which he had used to murder the victim. Some of the drawings contain apparently accurate details of the scene of the murder. At 12.30 am on Wednesday 11 October 1972 the appellant called the attention of the police and provided two further sheets of paper about which he was questioned. He described a wound on the face of the victim, and was asked about two drawings, one of a woman fully clothed and the other of a person without clothes. He said that the first one was after he and the victim had rolled about on the ground and the other how he had left the victim under the hedge. Asked why he had drawn no face in the second picture he said that the victim had been lying on her tummy and he seemed to remember that she had no clothes on. The appellant was not cautioned on this occasion. At about 7am on the same day he was taken back to Tamworth.

There, at 8.50am, he was interviewed by two Detective Chief Superintendents. At the outset of the interview he was fully and properly cautioned. In the course of the interview he gave answers which, on their face, implicated him as the murderer. For example, he described intimate details of the victim's personal appearance which anyone who had not witnessed the scene would have been most unlikely to know, unless told. In the course of the interview he took one of his Valium tablets.

Following this interview, the appellant readily agreed to accompany a Detective Sergeant of the Metropolitan Police on a tour to reconstruct the route which the appellant had followed on the day of the murder. He said:

> 'I want all this cleared up. If I don't receive some treatment I may do it again. I don't want that to happen.'

In the course of this tour the appellant went, with the police officer, from the barracks to Robinson's Field. The appellant then showed the police officer the route which he said he had taken, expressing difficulty in remembering certain physical features, but showing considerable certainty about others. The route indicated by the appellant suggested to the officer that, although some details of the scene had changed as a result of the change of season between June and October, the appellant had a clear recollection of the route he had taken at the time. It does not, however, appear that the officer made any notes of the interview at the time, and the appellant had the benefit of no advice during this reconstruction.

At 3.10pm that same day the appellant was taken from his cell and further interviewed by the Detective Chief Superintendents who did not on this occasion caution him. He repeated much of what he had said before. When it was suggested to him that the victim's bicycle had been found nowhere near the body the appellant strongly contradicted the officer, suggesting that he had put the bicycle in the hedge near the body and he could remember the seat and handlebars sticking out. In fact, as found, the seat and handlebars of the bicycle did not stick out. The appellant was questioned in detail about his earlier drawings and writings. At the end of this interview the appellant made a signed statement under caution. In this he clearly implicated himself as the murderer. Many of the details in this statement accorded with the facts as then known or later established, but some did not.

On the following day, 12 October 1972, having been cautioned, the appellant readily agreed to a further tour of the scene of the murder, this time accompanied by a photographer. He said:

> 'I told you. I killed her, I don't want it to happen again. I'll help you all I can, you must believe me now. I've told you what I did.'

A further visit was then made to the scene of the murder, including the route from the barracks to Robinson's Field [*sic*], and photographs were taken of the appellant pointing out the route to the police officer. There has never been any challenge to the accuracy of the police officer's account of this reconstruction, but again it appears that no note was made of what had transpired until afterwards and again the appellant had the benefit of no advice at the time. At 5pm on that date he was visited by his mother, who expressed disbelief that he could have been involved in this murder. He insisted that he had been. At 5.50pm on the same day he was formally arrested for murder and cautioned. When charged with the murder at 6.15pm and cautioned he replied 'Yes' and after a pause 'I did it'. He then added:

'These drawings and writing I did for you, I want used in evidence.'

While in custody awaiting trial, the appellant was the subject of detailed medical investigation. Dr J F Scott, a consultant psychiatrist, wrote:

'I could find no evidence of aggression nor viciousness in this boy's make-up. He showed no evidence of quick temper and appeared anxious to volunteer as much information as he could remember. In the circumstances, I feel that an abreaction would be valuable and might reveal more accurately the areas, in which he claims that he has forgotten what occurred and might produce evidence that would be valid in respect of the girl, who was so tragically murdered.'

The appellant was interviewed by Dr Washbrook, the prison medical officer at Winson Green. He described the excitement and sense of self-importance which the appellant had experienced when the police first challenged the answers given in the proforma, which appeared to be a highlight in the appellant's life. The doctor recorded:

'At one stage I suggested to him that were I to let him go home and that he would be free to do so with the charge dropped what would his reactions be. At this he said that he would be very perplexed since he needs to know in his own mind if he did or did not commit the offence, and that the burden on his mind of this indecision would make life intolerable. He stressed his need to know the truth which to him is important subjectively.'

The doctor's opinion was:

> 'As far as his memory is concerned for immediate, recent and remote events it was normal excepting the period of the day connected with the offence. Here it is very difficult to get any absolute impression but it would seem that at the present time he does have this defect of memory, probably hysterical in origin for the events that occurred on that particular day. The defect is somewhat patchy and its extent does fluctuate from time to time but the recall of essential details connected with the offence he was not able to supply. He is well orientated for time, place and person. His insight is normal and his judgement unimpaired.'

In a later report the doctor diagnosed an amnesia located in the afternoon and evening when the alleged offence was said to have occurred. He expressed the view that something occurred at that time which was such as to cause a 'disassociation', probably hysterical in origin, which befitted the appellant's personality and necessitated the true facts being pushed into the unconscious and being then incapable of recall to the realm of the conscious. He continued:

> 'It is also conceivable that nothing particularly significant happened on the day in question, which although it was the day prior to his leaving the Army, fitted well into the routine pattern of a young, serving soldier's life. This being so, the intervention in his life of an interview situation at the home of his grandmother by the police, in a vulnerable personality, could have triggered off a series of psychic reactions. This psychological set could evoke a

recall defect associated with the reproduction of falsified memories which would be without apparent provisional motivation to himself, other than his being brought into the limelight.'

Those who examined the appellant increasingly came to the view that he was suffering from amnesia, an unconscious mental mechanism by which painful or horrific events were obliterated from memory. In order to try and search the appellant's recollection, it was decided to administer barbiturate drugs and then question the appellant firmly at a time when his unconscious inhibitions would be reduced. The first of these abreaction sessions took place on Friday 30 March 1973, very shortly before the appellant's trial began. Under the influence of the drug, the appellant at first insisted that he had remained in the barracks all day, but went on to say that he could vaguely remember 'pictures'. He repeated again and again that he saw a body with legs flexed and exposed and a man standing over the body, whom the appellant described. He spoke of barbed wire and a sign low down and remembered the name 'Brookes'. For quite long periods he would repeat continually 'I don't know', 'I don't know' and 'I didn't do it', 'I didn't do it' and 'I must find out' and 'Was it me?'

The second abreaction session was conducted on 2 April 1973, just before the trial opened. On this occasion an initial injection of Brietal was followed by administration of Methedrine, intended to cause a general arousal of thoughts and recall. On this occasion the appellant again said that he had not left the barracks but went on to say that he was familiar with the geographic area where the offence had allegedly been committed because previously he had been there during his training and also because he had been taken there by the police. He was emphatic in saying that he had not murdered the victim. He repeatedly said that he had never seen the victim nor had he killed her and that if he disliked someone his normal reaction would be to run away from the scene.

Following these two sessions, Dr Washbrook opposed the conduct of a third session, which he felt would be harsh on the appellant and unlikely to produce results of value. A third session was, however, conducted, on Saturday 7 April 1973, during the trial and only two days before the appellant himself gave evidence. He gave a description of the man whom he said he had seen standing over the body of the victim. Following this session Dr Washbrook's opinion was:

(i) The defect of recall is not a true amnesia of hysterical disassociation.
(ii) The argument as to the element of malingering as opposed to hysteria is ruled out here by the patchy recall and the persistence of certain factors throughout the three closely placed sessions under drugs.
(iii) The recall is distorted to such a state that it is paramnesia more than true amnesia and that there is a falsification of recall and almost a delusional quality about certain aspects of it.
(iv) The factors which recur without alteration or a great deal of distortion would serve as some possible element of truth for remembering.

At the trial, the appellant's primary defence was one of alibi: that he had remained in the barracks all day and had never been in the vicinity of the scene of the murder. He was, however, unable to call any evidence in support of this defence, and in the course of his own evidence acknowledged that he might have been in the area of the field where, it appeared, the murder had been committed. It was no doubt in the light of this answer that three doctors were called to give evidence of the appellant's mental state.

The first of these witnesses, Dr Anton Stephens, gave it as his opinion that the appellant had no memory of the events connected with the murder of the victim and no memory of his personal involvement. His diagnosis was that the appellant suffered from amnesia, caused by emotional shock which caused suppression of traumatic recollections. He continued:

> 'Either the defendant did kill Judith Roberts or [that] he witnessed the killing and events connected with it, and that [that] in itself was sufficient a shock to have caused the memory suppression.'

Asked whether it was possible for the appellant to have imagined his involvement in the killing without having had any involvement, he answered that it was 'just possible'. He expressed the clear opinion that the appellant had been present at the scene of the killing. Dr Bluglass, called by the Crown, agreed that hysterical amnesia could have been caused in the appellant either by his guilt at having committed the crime or by his coming across the body.

Dr Washbrook, called by the defence, and basing himself on examination of the appellant alone, thought that his inability to remember was genuine. He agreed that shock was a possible cause of amnesia and thought the most likely explanation of the appellant's amnesia was his awareness of what had occurred at the murder scene.

Very early in his direction to the jury, the trial judge said:

'Now in this case you are faced with a problem. There is no question here that Evans is insane. No doctor suggests that he is or that he is what is described as diminished responsibility, that is to say, some mental disorder which reduces his liability from murder to manslaughter. What is said though is, and it is said by 3 doctors who agree that there is amnesia, that he has forgotten certain painful facts. That is what the doctors think, and the doctors are working on the assumption that Evans is wrong when he says that he never left the barracks on the 7th June and that at some stage he must have been in Robinson's field at a time when that girl's body, whether she was dead or dying, was there, and Mr Owen is perfectly right in saying to you that if you come to the conclusion that it may be that he was in Robinson's field and saw someone else injuring that girl, that would not be sufficient to convict him of murder. You have got to be satisfied that he killed that girl and caused her death before you can convict him of murder. Right?

Now if he did, the fact that he has forgotten parts of the facts or that he forgets a great deal is no defence, because, as you have heard from the doctors, people do do acts, criminal acts, cruel acts, and within a very short time afterwards there is a mechanism of the mind which draws a veil over the painful and shaming acts that they have done and causes them to forget quite genuinely many parts, if not the whole, of that which they have done, but that does not excuse. It is not a defence. If it is established to the satisfaction of the jury that a person kills another and that he does it with the intention that I have indicated to you, either to kill or to cause really serious injury, then the fact that he has forgotten all about it does not avail him as a defence to murder. I want to make that perfectly clear to you.'

Going on to give a brief summary of the appellant's defence the judge said:

'The defence is: I did not assault or kill that girl. I do not remember if I was present at that field or not at the time that the girl's body was there, and, as he told you in his evidence in chief, I do not remember leaving the barracks that day and did not leave the barracks that day, and Mr Owen, basing his argument on the evidence of the doctors, relies on Dr Stephens who says that from the account given by the defendant he favours the view that the defendant looked into the field, saw a crime committed by someone else and occluded if from his mind and that there was with a great deal of partial recall together with a great deal of fantasy when he came to make those statements and, as I say to you, in summarising the case for the Crown and the case for the defence, unless you are convinced on the evidence that the accused did kill the girl and meant either to kill her or cause grievous bodily harm, you must acquit.'

The judge then reminded the jury of the detailed evidence, drawing their attention to the facts relied on by the prosecution to show that the appellant had committed the murder and scrupulously pointing out the inaccuracies in the appellant's statements, relied on by the defence as showing that he had not committed the murder. He reminded the jury of the appellant's alibi, but also reminded them of a letter which the appellant had written to Dr Washbrook on Sunday 8 April, the day after the third abreaction session and the day before the appellant gave evidence. In this letter the appellant wrote:

> 'I am sure that I told the police that I had killed this girl, I cannot actually remember telling the police. I cannot remember the thoughts that were in my mind. I remember the drawings, the drawing parts, not all. I am anxious to know whether I was connected with the death of the girl. I know I have not done it. When I told the police that I had killed the girl I believed that was the truth, I never said that it was not the field. I never said that the field was rough. I was trying to impress on the police that I had killed this girl. I do not know why.'

The jury convicted. The appellant did not seek leave to appeal, and for many years following his conviction accepted without reservation his responsibility for this murder. It was only in 1991, apparently prompted by a casual observation during a home leave, that the appellant began to assert his innocence. The result of this change of stance for him personally was highly disadvantageous since he was at once returned to closed prison conditions.

In the course of this hearing, no criticism has been made of the trial judge, who took obvious pains to sum up the case in a fair and even-handed way. Equally, no criticism has been made of trial counsel, who had an extremely difficult defence to conduct; he was bound to advance the appellant's alibi defence, but the weakness of that defence was obvious and counsel skilfully [sic] relied on the contention that, even if the appellant had been present at the scene of the murder, he had not himself committed the crime. In the light of the medical evidence then available to the defence, it is hard to see what other defence could have been advanced. Judged by the rules and standards of today, the conduct of this investigation by the police left much to be desired: the appellant was not cautioned as and when he should have been, as is accepted by the Crown, he was not seen by a doctor when he first appeared at the police station, although it is clear that by current standards medical attention was urgently required; he was not offered the assistance of a solicitor. No complaint whatever was, however, made at the time of the police conduct of this investigation. It would seem that the main reason why the police were slow to caution, arrest and charge the appellant was their initial skepticism about the reliability of his account. It seems likely that, particularly to begin with, the police suspected the appellant of being mentally deranged. Our overall impression is that they treated him with sympathy and understanding, even though there were a number of respects in which the procedure adopted would not satisfy modern standards.

In arguing that this conviction is unsafe, the central thrust of Mr O'Connor's argument is that the case against the appellant rested on his own uncorroborated confession. That confession, it is submitted, must now be regarded as wholly unreliable. The diagnosis upon which the doctors relied at the trial, amnesia prompted by the experience of painful and horrific events, can no longer be accepted as correct. The appellant's conviction could only be supported now it if were possible for the court properly to conclude that there were facts known to the appellant, not deriving from any external source, which only the murderer could have known. But that, Mr O'Connor argues, is a conclusion not now open to this court, since the issues as presented to the jury at the trial did not call for exploration and decision as they would have done if the present issue had been that which the jury had to resolve.

It is correct that the prosecution case against the appellant at trial rested entirely on his own confessions. There was no identification evidence against him (although a soldier in uniform, wandering about the lanes and field on his own, might have been expected to attract attention). There was no scientific evidence of any kind to link him with the crime. The driver of the van in which the appellant claimed to have been given a lift never came forward. When he handed in his uniform on the day after the killing no stains were seen.

We must also accept that the appellant's confessions were as confessions, entirely unreliable. Such was the consensus among four very distinguished experts called to give evidence before us. While these experts did not enjoy the advantage enjoyed by the Doctors who testified at the trial of examining the appellant within months of this offence, they were at one in regarding the diagnosis of amnesia as unsound. In a written report dated 16 October 1997 provided by Dr Joseph, a consultant forensic psychiatrist instructed by the Crown, the matter is put in this way:

> 'I believe that when the appellant was in the police station on Monday, 9th October 1972 onwards, he was in a highly abnormal mental state. When he described "seeing" the face of the dead girl I believe he is describing what would be categorised as a pseudo-hallucination, namely an abnormal perceptual experience, which is not associated with a psychotic process, for example schizophrenia, but is associated with what can be described as a hysterical state. I believe that the appellant was in a markedly anxious and "hysterical" frame of mind and it is not

uncommon in such a state for a sufferer to believe that they can see things. It is of particular note that the appellant kept thinking that he was going mad and this is also a common symptom.

Taking into account the appellant's abnormal mental state and the way he was presenting himself at the police station, if I had been the psychiatrist examining him at that time or soon afterwards, I would have started off from the basic premise that the "memory" and imagery that he was describing were false and not true. I believe however that the psychiatrists who saw him at that time started from the opposite premise, namely that the memory and imagery the appellant was describing were true but incomplete. I believe that this assumption was also held by the police officers in the case and would undoubtedly have been conveyed to the appellant, who, in his desperate search for understanding of what was happening to him and his belief that he was going mad, is likely to have believed that there were gaps in his memory which he tried to fill by confabulating.

In a sense, I believe the police and the appellant were operating from different agendas, the police were trying to establish whether the appellant had been involved in the crime, the appellant, on the other hand, was trying to reassure himself that he was not going mad and was also desperate for attention and the need to be cared for. He was also a guilt-ridden youth, particularly regarding sexual matters, who, because of his own sense of worthlessness and self-hatred, seems to have assumed, that he must have killed the girl. I think both the agendas of the police and the appellant were satisfied by the appellant admitting his involvement in the murder of Judith Roberts.

In conclusion, therefore, from a psychiatric point of view, the appellant was in a highly abnormal state at the time of his confession to the murder of Judith Roberts. He has a tendency to confabulate to fill in gaps in his memory, and the effect of psychiatric intervention at that time was to reinforce the belief that he was suppressing a real memory rather than what I believe to have been the correct analysis, namely that he had been experiencing a pseudo hallucination and false memory as part of his extreme anxiety and "hysterical" state, which he subsequently elaborated with police and psychiatric encouragement. I believe therefore that his confession is unreliable.'

None of the doctors who have examined the appellant, whether in 1972–73 or more recently, has considered that the appellant was pretending to be unable to remember that which he did remember. They did not consider that he was feigning an inability to remember. In Dr Joseph's opinion, acceptance that the appellant did not know if he had committed the killing led to acceptance that he had not done the killing since if he had done it he would be aware of it. Once the diagnosis of amnesia triggered by emotional shock is rejected, the simple dichotomy put to the jury (that the appellant had either committed the killing or witnessed it) becomes unsustainable.

On behalf of the Crown, Mr Bruce Houlder QC presented his case with conspicuous moderation and judgement. He readily accepted that in various respects the investigative procedures adopted fell short of what would now be required. He did not challenge the strong criticism advanced by the doctors of the use of abreaction techniques as a means of eliciting the truth in a case such as this, the third session conducted in the course of the trial being particularly objectionable because of the risk that the subject might repeat that which had been strongly suggested to him under the influence of drugs. Mr Houlder did, however, submit, even accepting the unreliability of the appellant's confessions as confessions, that they contained information inconsistent with any explanation other than the guilt of the appellant as murderer. In support of this submission Mr Houlder very properly relied in particular on certain intimate details relating to the body of the victim and on the appellant's apparently reliable recollection of certain physical features in the vicinity of Robinson's field [*sic*]. These were formidable points, the effect of which cannot be lightly dismissed. If, to allow the appeal, we were required to be satisfied of the appellant's innocence, we would not be so satisfied. But that is not our task. Under section 2(1)(a) of the Criminal Appeal Act 1968 we are required to allow an appeal against conviction if we think that the conviction is unsafe. That requires us to consider whether we are satisfied the appellant was rightly convicted.

While accepting that in certain compelling circumstances a defendant may be convicted on the basis of knowledge not obtainable from extraneous sources which only the perpetrator of a crime could have acquired, Mr O'Connor submitted that that stringent test was not satisfied by the evidence in this case. He pointed out that many of the interviews relied upon by the Crown were not recorded contemporaneously, and furthermore that there was no comprehensive record of what had passed between the appellant and police officers nor of times at which casual conversations could have taken place. He moreover relied on inconsistencies between the true facts and the appellant's account as throwing doubt on the cogency of the knowledge relied upon. Our attention was drawn, for example, to the apparent unreliability of the appellant's account of the direction from which the victim had been cycling; to the absence of corroboration, on the victim's body or on her shoes, of the appellant's account of dragging her from the road over rough surfaces to the field; to his account of her continuing to struggle when the medical evidence suggested that the first blow, struck when the victim was upright, had been fatal and rendered her unconscious; to the appellant's suggestion that he had struggled with the victim on the far side of the field, about sixty yards distant from where her body was found; to doubts about his account of the weapons he had used in the course of the attack; to his suggestion on some occasions that he had left the body unclothed; to the absence of any explanation about how and when the victim's bicycle had been moved into the field; to his incorrect description of what could be seen of the bicycle as it lay in the hedge; to his incorrect statement that he had placed the victim's shoes inside her underclothes; to the absence of any reference to covering the body with hedge cuttings and blue plastic fertiliser bags; to the failure to identify the green van in which the appellant claimed to have been given a lift; to the absence of any sighting of the appellant, in uniform, in the field or on the road; to errors in the appellant's description of the victim's personal appearance and dress; and to contradictions in the appellant's own accounts given from time to time.

We have found this an extremely difficult and anxious appeal to resolve. All now depends on whether we can be sure that information vouchsafed by the appellant to the police, insofar as it was accurate, was information which the appellant could only have acquired by virtue of his being the murderer. That, however, was not the issue which the jury had to resolve. Because of the choice then put before them, that (leaving the obviously suspect alibi on one side) the appellant had either committed the murder or been present at the scene, it was plainly unnecessary to investigate with any rigour the sources of the appellant's knowledge, since he could have acquired most if not all of that knowledge on either hypothesis. This meant that while the sources of his knowledge were an issue at the trial, they were not (as now) the issue. Had they been the issue, we have no doubt that all possible sources of the appellant's allegedly incriminating knowledge would have been minutely scrutinised, and very close attention paid to all possible communications between the appellant and the officers in whose custody he was for several vital days.

Such scrutiny and examination might no doubt have proved sufficient to support the prosecution case. Some consideration was given at the trial to press and television coverage as a potential source of the appellant's information. However, the meticulously fair summing-up made no reference to this coverage, not even to the information given in the only television report the appellant said he saw, to the effect that the bicycle was found near the body. This detracted from the apparently persuasive effect of the appellant's insistence as to the location of the bicycle near the body. But it is in our judgement impossible for this court, in the absence of full scrutiny and examination, now to be sure. These matters were never explored before the jury as they would have been had the case as it now is been that which the jury had to decide. Given the obvious caution which is needed before convicting a defendant on this ground, we do not now conclude that it would be safe for us to base our conclusion on matters never fully explored before the jury.

Mr O'Connor challenged the conviction on certain additional grounds, contending that the appellant's confessions were (because of the procedures adopted) inadmissible, that the expert medical witnesses in their evidence exceeded the proper bounds of expert evidence, that the trial judge misdirected the jury on the standard of proof and that there was evidence of an unidentified fingerprint (not belonging to the appellant) found on the victim's bicycle in the course of the murder inquiry. We have the gravest doubt whether any of these grounds, viewed singly or cumulatively, would cause us to doubt the safety of this conviction, and some of the points made seem highly debatable. It is however unnecessary for us to review these grounds in detail, having regard to the conclusion which we have already reached and expressed.

For reasons already given, we conclude that this conviction is unsafe and we accordingly allow the appeal and quash the conviction.

Having heard the evidence, the judges were critical of the manner in which the police inquiry was conducted. It was said that during his questioning, Evans was offered no medical assistance, despite his mental and physical condition. Police also did not offer Evans access to a solicitor, and often failed to caution him as procedure required. O'Connor said that Evans' confession would not have been given had a doctor or solicitor been present because he would have been diagnosed as unfit to be interviewed.

On the question of the content of his statement, Lord Bingham said,

> In this he clearly implicated himself as the murderer. Many of the details in this statement accorded with the facts as then known or later established, but some did not.

The judges held that psychiatric testimony at the original trial was unreliable, and a doctor told the appeal Evans had suffered 'false memory' as a result of the extreme anxiety and hysterical state he was in at the time. Because of his state of mind, the confession would not have been admissible under the law as it stood in 1997. The Court also heard that none of Judith's blood had been found on Evans, and a fingerprint on her bike did not belong to him. The Court consequently quashed Evans' conviction after deeming it to be unsafe, and he was released from custody with immediate effect.

At the time of his release, the twenty-five years Evans had spent in jail was the longest period served by an individual in the United Kingdom as the result of a miscarriage of justice, though in 2001 it would be surpassed by the twenty-seven years served by Stephen Downing following his wrongful conviction of the murder of Wendy Sewell.

Following the appeal, Staffordshire Police said that they had no plans to reopen their investigation into the murder of Judith Roberts, as all lines of inquiry had been exhausted at the time. A spokesman also stated that investigators had followed correct procedure,

> and there was never any question of misconduct by any of those officers.

Evans sought compensation from the Home Office for his wrongful conviction, and in 2000 was awarded £750,000. Together with other payments he received from them, his solicitor estimated the total amount of his compensation was around one million pounds. The sum was the largest award made in the United Kingdom to a person who has suffered a miscarriage of justice. Speaking of his compensation, Evans said,

> For the past two and a half years we have been fighting for this money and at last it has been sorted. I am relieved. I will never be fully free – every time I lock a door I have flashbacks to being in prison.

The *Daily Star* reported on Friday, 9 June 2000 on page two:

> A man wrongly convicted at 17 of the murder of a Schoolgirl was yesterday awarded almost £750,000. Andrew Evans was sentenced to life in 1972 for the murder of 14-year-old Judith Roberts, who was battered to death near her home in Tamworth, Staffs. Mr Evans, now 45, had been on medication at the time of the murder and went to see police because he had dreamt of a girl's face. Asked if he had killed Judith, he said: 'I don't know.' The bizarre 'confession' – the only real evidence – was accepted by a jury. In 1994 Mr Evans began a campaign to prove his innocence. He was freed in 1997.

Chapter Eleven

Other Murders Involving a Walling Hammer

Murders committed upon females in Staffordshire from three years prior to Judith Roberts' murder were rare and comprised of one domestic-related case; that of Roland William Edwards, who killed his wife, Patricia Edwards, on 29 December 1969 at Coseley, Dudley. The cause of death was ruled as suffocation. Edwards was convicted of manslaughter. Aside from this, the only other murders committed were male on male, including the case of Alan Peter Lakin who killed his brother, Maurice John Lakin, on 21 August 1971 at Tamworth by stabbing him with a kitchen knife. Following consideration of the evidence, the justices found insufficient evidence to commit for trial. Another known case, unlike the aforementioned, did not involve the killing of a family member. David Sharratt, a mental patient, was convicted of murdering Colin Machin on 24 February 1972 in Clayton by stabbing him. There were no unsolved cases within the county to compare with Judith's case. In the neighbouring county of Stoke-on-Trent, one case still unsolved is the 1973 murder of Mary Ann Armstrong. A known sex worker aged 32, she was murdered on 24 March 1973 in a car park in Hanley. She was stabbed to death. The *Birmingham Daily Post* reported the week after she was killed:

> [that she was a] lonely prostitute who used to tell men she had eight children in an effort to get drinks from them and play on their sympathy.

Leading the manhunt for Armstrong's killer was DCS Terrance O'Connor of New Scotland Yard, who described the individual as 'probably mentally sick'. There was a fear that the perpetrator may strike again.

A man named Donat Gomez was charged and later acquitted in May 1974 after a trial lasting sixty-three days. Within the bordering police force areas there were a number of unsolved murders which we believe may prove to be connected to Judith's, which we will examine here. These cases were highlighted in *Yorkshire Ripper – The Secret Murders: The True Story of Serial Killer Peter Sutcliffe's Reign of Terror* by Chris and Tim. The book, originally published in 2015, connected the following cases which still remain unsolved:

Carol Wilkinson

As previously stated in Chapter Nine, the murder of Jean Jordan was committed on Saturday, 1 October 1977 and, in fact, hers connects Sutcliffe even more to Judith's murder than is immediately noticeable. That same year another murder took place in Bradford; it was just days after Jean was killed by Sutcliffe. What's more, the murder occurred during the day he had returned to her body to further desecrate it. On Monday, 10 October 1977, sometime between 9.00 and 9.30 am, 20-year-old Carol Wilkinson was savagely attacked as she walked from her home at 131 Ranelagh Avenue to her place of work at Bradford Bakery in Gain Lane, Fagley. It was an approximately fifteen-minute walk from her house to the bakery. Carol had not been able to catch the bus to work that day because there was a bus strike.

A male hospital cook called Stephen Smith, who may have disturbed her attacker, found Carol lying in a pool of blood behind the bakery. She was beaten about the back of her head, by what the police described as a large 56lb coping stone and was partially stripped. We believe that this was in fact a walling hammer, and as a rock found nearby had Carol's blood on it, the police – not for the first time – concluded that that was the murder weapon. This was also the case in Yvonne Pearson's murder, committed on 21 January 1978, until Sutcliffe confessed that he had used a walling hammer while carrying out her murder.

Her trousers and pants had been pulled down and her bra lifted up; it would appear that the offender had been disturbed during the attack. When found, Carol was barely alive and taken to hospital, where tests showed that she had multiple skull fractures and severe brain damage. She was immediately put on a life support machine. Two days later, on 12 October 1977, doctors sadly concluded that her brain had ceased to function and the life support machine was switched off. This attack, although carried out on a daylight morning, has some glaring similarities to that of the murder of Yvonne Pearson, which was committed just three months later. Police considered that Yvonne's attacker had used a boulder rather than a hammer. Later that year, Professor Gee, the Home Office pathologist who conducted all the postmortem examinations on Sutcliffe's victims, noted that there were similarities between the murders of Carol and Yvonne. Sutcliffe did not confess to Carol's murder at his Old Bailey trial. But at the time of her death, his home was just over 3 miles from the Bradford bakery. Peter and Sonia Sutcliffe had moved into their new home in Garden Lane, Heaton on Monday, 26 September 1977. Sutcliffe had also changed his vehicle. Having sold his white Ford Corsair – which had been used in many of the previous attacks and murders – he had bought the same model, this time in red. In addition, his place of work was approximately 2.5 miles from the bakery.

As was the case with Judith's murder, a miscarriage of justice occurred when, eighteen months later, a man named Anthony Steel was charged with Carol Wilkinson's murder. He served two decades behind bars for a crime that he did not commit, until the conviction was finally quashed in February 2003 by the Court of Appeal due to new evidence from both defence and Crown consultant psychologists, which indicated that:

> [Steel] is, and was, mentally handicapped and at the borderline of abnormal suggestibility and compatibility. He was therefore a significantly more vulnerable interviewee than could be appreciated at the time of the trial.

Anthony's release from prison was bitter-sweet; he was a free man, and when his conviction was overturned he received an official police apology and a compensation pay-out from the government of £100,000, but he and his family had suffered immensely from the ordeal, and only four years after his release, Anthony suffered a fatal heart attack, dying prematurely at the age of 52 on 29 September 2007. The effect of the miscarriage of justice and his death, coupled with the incompetence of the police when investigating Anthony, had an irreversible effect on his family. Their understandable anger at West Yorkshire Police for the years Anthony lost and the death he ultimately suffered is still felt today.

Anthony Steel was eliminated as a suspect, which begs the question: who killed Carol? A woman, who was then a teenager, living on Carol's estate, opposite her house, claims that the year before Carol's murder – during the long hot summer of 1976 – her stepdad's large chest freezer had broken down and that Peter Sutcliffe arrived and fixed it. She and other witnesses recalled that they saw Sutcliffe hanging around the estate, in particular on Langdale Road, during February 1977, and that it was reported to the local police at the time. There are further claims that George Wilkinson, Carol's father, chased Sutcliffe off the estate on a number of occasions after attempts to court his daughter. All in all, with the method of the attack and Sutcliffe's likely disposition during the early hours of the morning of 10 October 1977 (i.e. angry and frustrated at not finding the £5 note on Jean Jordan's body) coupled with the information of witnesses putting him on the estate where Carol lived, he has to be a strong candidate for the culprit who killed Carol.

Wendy Sewell

Less than three years after the murder of Barbara Mayo, another notable Derbyshire murder took place, approximately 12 miles away, and set in motion what would become the biggest miscarriage of justice in British history. While the murders of Jacqui Ansell-Lamb and Barbara Mayo were almost identical, the same can be said for the murders of Wendy Sewell and Judith Roberts. It was at around midday on Wednesday, 12 September 1973 that Wendy Sewell, a 32-year-old married woman who worked as a secretary for the local Forestry Commission, left her office in Bakewell. Wendy's life in the months leading up to her death had been turbulent. She had left her husband, David Sewell, for a lover. The pair had reconciled, but on the condition that Wendy – who had fallen pregnant – gave up the child she had conceived with the other man. Wendy agreed, and she and David had been piecing their marriage back together in the aftermath of infidelity. The afternoon she was murdered, Wendy was to visit the nearby cemetery to look at graves to help her mother decide on the headstone for Wendy's father, who had recently died. Just before she left the office, Wendy had scribbled a note and left it with her boss in an adjoining office while he was on the phone. Before she left the building, the employer heard her in her office talking to an unknown man, who spoke with an abrupt high-pitched voice.

It is worth noting that while Peter Sutcliffe's first official attack – and his first confirmed murder victim – wasn't until 1975, his criminal record shows that he committed assaults as early as 1969, when he attacked a woman in Bradford with a piece of brick encased in a sock, which he smashed across the back of her head. Tracy Browne, a survivor of an attack by Sutcliffe, and former taxi driver John Tomey – who claims he was attacked by Sutcliffe in 1969 after he picked him up in his cab in Leeds city centre – both remarked on his insipid high-pitched voice when they encountered him. Several witnesses would recall seeing Wendy enter the local cemetery off Yeld Road at approximately 12.50 pm, one of whom being 17-year-old cemetery worker Stephen Downing, who was about to go home for a quick break from tending the local garden. His plan was to return twenty minutes later after buying lemonade from a local shop, but the shop was shut and so, according to Stephen, after he returned home he asked his mother to drop the lemonade off to him at the cemetery later, once the shop had opened. It is estimated that during the fifteen-minute window between Stephen leaving the cemetery and returning, Wendy was subjected to a frenzied attack. Bakewell Cemetery is split into two chapels. The first, situated closest to the gate, is the consecrated chapel. A second chapel, the unconsecrated, was further into the graveyard, and home to the chapel workers' tool shed.

As Wendy wandered along on the footpath in the cemetery close to the consecrated chapel, her attacker pounced. Marks on her knees would suggest she was standing when she was attacked, the first injury supposedly a ligature wrapped around her neck, which brought her to her knees. It would appear that, after she was attacked, Wendy's body was dragged 25 feet in order to conceal her in rough ground amongst old headstones on the Catcliffe Wood side of the cemetery; again, this was a common MO of Sutcliffe. Concealed from the view of passersby, Wendy was struck over the back of her head at least eight times with a pickaxe handle. The large and heavy weapon would need a strong person to wield it at shoulder height in order to execute the blows that Wendy sustained. Her killer acted in broad daylight and they acted quickly, removing her plimsolls, trousers, knickers and tights; her blouse and bra were lifted upwards in a similar method seen in

Sutcliffe's attacks, which would begin to be catalogued just two years later. We believe that the interference with the victim's clothing was in preparation for her attacker to stab and slash at her breasts and abdomen – something Sutcliffe had similarly done to survivors Anna Rogulskyj and Olive Smelt in 1975. Both women were left with slash marks on their bodies, Anna on her stomach, Olive on her back and buttocks.

However, it appears that Wendy's attacker was disturbed. A witness close to the scene on that day, on their lunchtime break, described seeing a man was seen running out of the cemetery up Butts Road, covered in blood. Who was this man? Could he have been Wendy's killer? What other horrors might the person who attacked the innocent council worker have subjected her to while she lay helpless, had they not been spooked? A bloodstained and splintered pickaxe handle was discovered lying alongside Wendy's bloody garments, which proved that she was fully dressed before being struck on the head and then undressed whilst semi-conscious. Police alleged that the pickaxe used to kill Wendy had come from an unlocked groundman's tool storage area in the unconsecrated chapel of the cemetery. An investigation twenty-five years later into Stephen Downing's confession found that the six assorted pickaxes and handles used by the cemetery workers – which were all stamped BUDC (Bakewell Urban District Council) – were all accounted for in the store. The murder weapon therefore had been brought to the cemetery by Wendy's attacker – but who was he? It would be revealed at his trial in 1981 that Sutcliffe had used a pickaxe in his two previous periods of employment with Bingley Cemetery and the Water Board. Also, he was a bodybuilder and had developed upper arm strength. Wendy was found a short while later by young Stephen.

Despite her injuries she was still alive – but barely. She was close to death. Determined to survive, Wendy stood up. Stephen recalls that she shook her head violently, splashing him with her blood before she staggered around before her legs buckled and she collapsed, hitting her already badly damaged skull on a gravestone. Stephen summoned help very quickly and Wendy was rushed to Chesterfield Royal Hospital by ambulance, where she was seen at 2.40 pm by a surgeon. Tests revealed that she had multiple lacerations of the skull, which an X-ray later confirmed were fractures.

Despite her brave attempt to survive the brutal attack, Wendy had lapsed into a coma. She died two days later without being able to reveal who had assaulted her.

Suspicion immediately fell on Stephen, who was arrested at the scene. While he was the prime suspect, Wendy's lovers were also suspected of her murder, as was her husband. It is clear from the injuries inflicted on the young woman that her killer was full of hate and rage for one reason or another. We believe that the police and the local population were looking inwardly and in the wrong direction for the perpetrator of this heinous crime, and that a compelling argument can be made that her killer was one Peter Sutcliffe. The day after Wendy's body succumbed to the horrific attack, on 15 September 1973, the Home Office pathologist found ten lacerations to the skull and concluded that she had been violently assaulted by someone using the pickaxe handle. There were seven or eight more violent blows, and whoever attacked Wendy would seem to have done so in a frenzied state. Stephen spent twenty-seven years behind bars for Wendy's murder. Following a successful appeal, a Derbyshire Police Public Enquiry (codenamed Operation Noble) was set up by the Chief Constable David Coleman during 2002.

Deputy Chief Constable Robert Wood OBE QPM was tasked with this, and his findings were released during 2003. This was a review that looked at all the facts of the original case. Wendy Sewell's murder was national news as was the injustice that followed, including the £1.8 million pay-out he received after a judge concluded that Stephen had spent twenty-seven years behind bars for a murder he was not responsible for. It was the longest miscarriage of justice in British legal history. Wendy's murder remains officially unsolved. Sutcliffe's use of a walling hammer in the murder of Yvonne Pearson in 1978 further links him to Carol Wilkinson and Judith Roberts. Regardless of the pathology report on Yvonne, police did not link Carol's death to Sutcliffe, but it begs the question: just how many men were there running around West Yorkshire banging women on the back of the head and then mutilating their bodies? The murder of Judith was very similar in nature to the other two miscarriage of justice cases outlined; a lone female attacked from behind with a blunt instrument, and lower clothing pulled down to expose the genitalia and top clothing to expose the breasts. In Judith's case it is apparent that she was smashed on the back of her head with a blunt instrument so heavy that it caused massive multiple fractures of the skull, which is identical to the cases of Carol and Yvonne.

Judith was dragged from the initial attack scene and hurriedly hidden in a nearby field entrance by covering her body with grass trimmings, plastic fertiliser sacks and a sheet of corrugated asbestos sheeting, which the pathologist wrongly concluded was the murder weapon. This is similar to Yvonne's murder, where she was clubbed with a heavy walling hammer, had her clothing disarranged and then hidden under soil, rubble and turf and an old, discarded sofa. The case is also similar to that of Wendy Sewell, where her head injuries were caused by a pickaxe handle after being attacked, she had been stupefied with a knotted garrote. Additionally, the nature of the crime was identical in that Wendy's clothing was disarranged in the same manner, and she was dragged from the initial attack scene. The two murders – committed in neighbouring police forces before and after the killing of Judith – were doggedly investigated on a parochial-based murder enquiry by Staffordshire Police, with the help of New Scotland Yard. At their disposal was the full expertise of New Scotland Yard murder squad, C11 criminal intelligence department and the various regional intelligence officers who looked at cross-border crimes and patterns. Teleprinter and *Police Gazette* circulations assisted, along with the method index, which compiled a list of all unsolved murders and offences against the person committed throughout the United Kingdom with a breakdown of the method employed. One such file was the arrest of Peter Sutcliffe and the use of a hammer, which was and still is a rarity as a choice of offensive weapon.

After Sutcliffe's arrest in January 1981, he was interviewed by DS Peter Smith and DI Boyle in the presence of his solicitor at Armley Prison. The topic turned to the use of a screwdriver by Sutcliffe during some of his attacks, namely those of Josephine Whittaker and Barbara Leach. Under the direction of Sutliffe, the officers drove to Woolley Edge Service Station off the M1 Motorway (Southbound). On the embankment near the services, the Western Area Task Force recovered a sharpened screwdriver with a wooden handle which Sutcliffe admitted he had thrown out of his lorry. After its retrieval, Sutcliffe was brought back to the prison. The officers hit 'record' on the interview tape and re-cautioned Sutcliffe. They spoke again about the screwdriver:

> DI Boyle: 'Was it your own screwdriver of the firms?'
> Sutcliffe: 'It was mane, an old one, I've had it in the garage for a long time.'
> DI Boyle: 'Can you describe it?'
> Sutcliffe: 'It had a wooden handle with the varnish worn off.'
> DI Boyle: 'Have you adapted it in any way?'
> Sutcliffe: 'I think I used it as a hole puncher for riveting. I sharpened it up with a grindstone.'
> DI Boyle: 'Would that alter the initial shape of the head?'
> Sutcliffe: 'Yes, it did, it was no good as it was for that job.'
> DI Boyle: 'What shape did it finish up?'
> Sutcliffe: 'It ended up sharp at the end.'

DI Boyle: 'What stone did you sharpen it on?'
Sutcliffe: 'Either the floor on the garage at home or with a Black and Decker carborundum, it altered it from a star shape to like a bradawl.'

Also when discussing the weapons Sutcliffe used, DI Boyle spoke of the murder of Yvonne Pearson in 1978.

DI Boyle: 'Did you kill Yvonne Pearson at Bradford?'
Sutcliffe: 'I did.'
DI Boyle: 'Is the version of that incident in your statement correct?'
Sutcliffe: 'Yes.'
DI Boyle: 'Before you covered her up, did you place something between her legs?'
Sutcliffe: 'No, I don't think so.'
DI Boyle: 'You describe the instrument on that occasion as a walling hammer. What do you mean by a walling hammer?'
Sutcliffe: 'It's like a lump hammer, a long oblong block on a nine-inch shaft...'
DI Boyle: 'What happened to that hammer?'
Sutcliffe: 'I honestly couldn't say, I thought it was in the garage.'

Chapter Twelve

Friday the 13th

The news that Sutcliffe had died came on a Friday; more fittingly, Friday, 13 November 2020. A day known for misfortune in the Western world, many would agree that the ending of Sutcliffe's life was not unfortunate in the slightest. We had an inkling that Sutcliffe's last days were upon him, as news had been circulating of his ill-health for a few months by this stage. In 2020, the world was gripped by a global pandemic, Covid-19. Prison officials would later reveal, at an inquest into the serial killer's death, that vulnerable prisoners at HMP Frankland where he was housed had been warned of the dangers of coronavirus after the first lockdown in March 2020. Prisoners were offered measures similar to shielding in the community, being kept apart from other inmates at mealtimes and when using the phone. Sutcliffe turned down the offer. He was not afraid of death; he had seen it firsthand in the most brutal of circumstances. The day before he died, author Chris was approached by journalists at Sky News for an interview about the serial killer, further sparking our feeling that someone, somewhere, knew Sutcliffe's life was coming to an end. It was reported in the media that the serial killer had been taken to hospital on 27 October 2020 after feeling dizzy and being diagnosed at the prison's healthcare unit with a blocked heart. Sutcliffe refused treatment and was on his way back to prison by 4 November 2020. With his diminished eyesight and overweight build, Sutcliffe was not in good shape, and it was obvious that the time left for him to confess to further murders was running out. The morning after Chris was approached for an interview the news came in: Sutcliffe was dead. The official cause was ruled as Covid-19, with heart disease and diabetes contributing. His death was not suspicious and was deemed to be from natural causes.

It has been more than four decades since Sutcliffe was arrested and later charged with the murders and attacks which saw him spend the rest of his life behind bars. He is now dead, unable to offer any shred of detail on any other crimes he may have committed. There can be little doubt that Sutcliffe did not go from living an ordinary life to suddenly attacking Anna Rogulskyj; serial killers by nature do not escalate to such violence without either a significant trauma or trigger, or unless they have been building up to it and their addiction has boiled over. Our belief that Sutcliffe was responsible for more crimes is unwavering; it is a belief brought about by years of research. It is not only our belief, but the belief of those who compiled The Byford Report in the aftermath of Sutcliffe's capture. It has now been more than fifty years since Judith was murdered. It's unfair that answers about who killed her are still to be found. We can only hope someone remembers something and can bring about a sense of closure to her family. Could there ever be justice done for Judith? There have been cold cases solved decades after their occurrence, some which seemed near impossible to solve but have been thanks to one piece of vital information.

In 2019, Seattle Police announced that a cold case, fifty-two years old, had finally been solved thanks to DNA technology. The victim, Susan Galvin, was a 20-year-old records clerk who had been raped and strangled in a parking garage elevator in 1967. Her killer was named Frank Wypych, a former soldier who had died in 1987. A perhaps better-known case is that of Joseph James DeAngelo, aka the 'Golden State Killer', which finally reached its conclusion in 2020, after more than thirty years since his last crime in California in 1986. DeAngelo was fortunately still alive, but now an old man; he was most likely only years from the grave and one step further removed from the crimes that devastated many.

With this in mind, we implore anyone who thinks they might know anything about Judith's murder to come forward and help see justice done. It is worth noting that in our research we found no other mention of possible theories as to who killed Judith.

Andrew Evans was quickly focused on by the police, and after his release from prison there doesn't seem to have been a renewed interest in the case.

No-one else has ever been questioned or charged other than Andrew, but after his acquittal there is no mention as to who else might be a suspect. Had other particular theories been presented, we feel it would have been only fair to mention them, but despite numerous appeals to retired officers, no one can recall any other theories surrounding Judith's murder. We can only wonder why new lines of enquiry were not looked into following Evans' release.

To that end, Chris sent the following FOI request to Staffordshire Police on 10 April 2022:

Dear Staffordshire Police,

You hold a file for Judith Roberts murder on 7th June 1972 in Wigginton. Could you please confirm:

a) That Judith's clothing was preserved and still held.

b) When was the last review of this case?

c) As it is coming up to 50 years whether the case will be reviewed with regards to testing the clothing with the new forensic and DNA techniques currently available, in order to identify a crime scene sample.

d) Whether any new crime scene sample will be tested against Andrew Evans's.

Yours faithfully,

Chris Clark

This was their reply:

FOI ref no: 14306 22nd April 2022 Freedom of Information request: reference 14306 first notified to us by email on 11th April 2022.

Thank you for your recent request under the Freedom of Information Act 2000, as detailed below:

'You hold a file for Judith Roberts murder on 7th June 1972 in Wigginton Could you please confirm:

a) That Judith's clothing was preserved and still held.

b) When was the last review of this case?

c) As it is coming up to 50 years whether the case will be reviewed with regards to testing the clothing with the new forensic and DNA techniques currently available, in order to identify a crime scene sample.

d) Whether any new crime scene sample will be tested against Andrew Evans's.

Staffordshire Police's response to your enquiry is as follows:

Staffordshire Police does hold some of the requested information.

Could you please confirm:

a) That Judith's clothing was preserved and still held In accordance with Section 17(1) of the Freedom of Information Act,

this letter represents a refusal notice for this question as Staffordshire Police can neither confirm nor deny that any it holds the information you requested as it believes the duty in sl(1)(a) of the Freedom of Information Act 2000 (the duty to confirm whether the public authority holds information of the specified description), does not apply, by virtue of the following exemptions: Section 30(3) – Criminal Investigations.

Section 30 is a class-based exemption and consideration must be given as to whether there is a public interest in neither confirming nor denying the information exists is the appropriate response. Factors favouring Confirming or Denying for Section 30 Confirming or denying whether information exists relevant to this request would lead to a better-informed general public identifying that the Staffordshire Police robustly investigate offences.

This would further promote public trust in providing transparency and demonstrating openness and accountability into where the police are currently focusing their investigations. Factors favouring Neither Confirming Nor Denying for Section 30 This relates to a murder investigation.

To confirm or deny whether or not the victim's clothing was held could hinder the prevention and detection of crime and cause offenders to take evasive action.

We were saddened when the fiftieth anniversary came and went without an appeal from Staffordshire Police for information. We waited to see Judith's name mentioned in the news, but nothing came. We approached Staffordshire Police for comment in June 2022, explaining the outline of the book and why we were looking at the case, and put the following questions to them:

What is the state of the case at present?

Was Peter Sutcliffe ever questioned about this case?

If so, what was the outcome of the enquiries?

Are Staffordshire Police still investigating this case?

Are any resources being dedicated to the case at present?

If so, is there any comment to be made on what those might be?

How does Staffordshire Police plan to address the unsolved nature of the case moving forward?

Is there likely to be a review of the evidence in Judith's case soon given that the case has surpassed a considerable amount of time without any new leads?

We gave them roughly a month's deadline to respond. Six minutes later we received the following comment:

The investigation has been subject to a number of formal independent reviews since the wrongful conviction and acquittal of Andrew Evans. Serious investigations of this nature remain under scrutiny, so when new information becomes available it is examined in the context of the overall case and every opportunity is exploited to bring offenders to justice.

Sutcliffe is now dead and unable to answer our burning question, but there is still hope that Judith's case can be solved. Many a cold case has gone unsolved for decades, with the killer finally being brought to justice. Unfortunately, if Sutcliffe was responsible for Judith's murder, he cannot be sentenced for it. When alive, Sutcliffe was already serving twenty concurrent life sentences. He was never going to be a free man and had spent years of his life being accused of additional crimes. He refused to crack, and had police not had him bang to rights on the murders and attacks he committed between 1975 and 1980 he would have no doubt denied his involvement on those too.

When undertaking research for this book, it became clear that the impact of Judith's murder is still felt within the community. When tracing classmates and school friends, many recalled the quiet girl and her twin sister, and for those who were close to her it is obvious that they've never forgotten her. Police still recall the investigation, even though the detectives are well into their retirement by now. The community remembers the 'soldier boy' who was convicted, and more than a fair few remarked how they didn't believe back then he had done it. Life has carried on, as it does when death and tragedy occur. However, we firmly believe that there is not an expiration date on truth and justice.

Appendix I

The expert pathologist's comments on Dr van der Merwe's findings and conclusions

> Re Judith Roberts deceased
> R v. Andrew James Evans
>
> I have studied the post-mortem report of Dr. Van der Merwe dated 28th June 1972, (p.40-48) and the report of Josceline Penelope Greenwood dated 2nd November 1972 (p.55-57).
>
> I have studied the albums of photographs Exhibits nos. G.H.1 and G.H.2.
>
> On Thursday 4th January 1973 at Tamworth Police Station in the presence of Chief Inspector Stewart and Detective Constable Maskery I examined the Exhibit Book listing all the exhibits in the case, as well as a number of selected exhibits, notably the alleged weapon ('F'), the clothing, the bicycle, and the hair.
>
> I took samples of asbestos from exhibit 'F' and took photographs of it. No wounds or pieces of bone were available for inspection.
>
> The following observations are made:
>
> 1. Eight exhibits (DX, DY, DZ, EA, EB, EC, ED and EE) comprising thirteen wounds or parts of wounds as well as several specimens of bone appear to have been submitted to the West Midland Forensic Science Laboratory.
>
> 2. There is no mention of these exhibits in Miss Greenwood's report. Presumably they are included in the last paragraph "...nothing of significance on any of the other articles I examined" (p.57).
>
> 3. Asbestos is a relatively soft material and fibres could be scraped from the raw margin of the alleged weapon with relative ease, although they were not plentiful in the scrapings when examined microscopically.
>
> 4. Human hairs resembling those of Judith Roberts ('AN' and 'AO') were plentiful in the fingers of the left hand (see 'Q'), the polythene bag 'AY', the privet cuttings 'AZ', and were found on asbestos 'D', although it is not suggested that 'D' was used as a weapon. That they were also found on the alleged weapon 'F' might only indicate chance contamination of this asbestos. They were obviously widely distributed. (Find out whether they were recovered from the bloodstained end, or from the surface. If the bloodstained end, this could

2.

mean no more than that the end was wet and sticky.)

5. By the same reasoning asbestos 'E' was stained with blood as well as the alleged weapon 'F'. The attack yielded much blood, the attacker's hand might have been bloodstained, and this hand might have contaminated the end of the asbestos 'F' in throwing it on to the body. (All three asbestos pieces were found on or alongside the body.)

6. The first blow, the main blow, the killing blow which was struck on the left hand side of the head was a very powerful downwards chop. If asbestos 'F' was used to produce the 11 cm. injury, it must have been brought down on its side edge, and not on its pointed edge. But the side edge is not apparently bloodstained, as the pointed end is.

7. Dr. Van der Merwe delayed his examination of the head for 10 days, from June 10th until June 20th. He will say that the delay was because the police were not sure what weapon had been used. Yet asbestos 'F' was found at the beginning of the enquiry, lying on the body.

8. The hair found in Judith's hand ('Q') is said to resemble that of Judith's head ('AN' and 'AO') but it has never been compared with that of the accused.

9. None of the wounds were examined microscopically or histochemically to ascertain if they were inflicted any reasonable time before death.

10. It is noted in the P.M. report that the wounds at the back of the head (photo 'P', exhibit G.H.1) had not bled and were therefore assumed to have been incurred 'after death'. Although the wounds on the front of the left hand side of the head (photo 'O' exhibit G.H.1) appeared to have bled, this could have been post-mortem bleeding, for they were 'dependent'. Post-mortem bleeding is very common. The corollary is that there could have been a significant lapse of time between the first fatal blow to the left hand side of the head and all the other blows being inflicted.

11. If the bone beneath the first fatal blow shows "a series of parallel scratches" (p.44, Dr. Van der Merwe) this could have been caused by the asbestos 'F', but it equally could have been caused by many rough weapons.

3.

Dr. Van der Merwe gives as the cause of death:

"A fractured skull,

due to blows to the head

with a sharp or partially pointed object".

It might be challenged whether asbestos 'F' is:

(1) Sufficiently sharp to have caused the major wound and <u>cut</u> the hairs found in many sites (p.56).

(2) Sufficiently heavy (2 lb., not 3 lb.) unless used as an axe, in which case the asbestos and not the skull <u>might</u> have broken (suggest obtaining similar sample and trying the effects of beating it on a table in Court).

(3) <u>Too clean on the edge</u> to have caused the major wound and

(4) perhaps <u>insufficient</u>ly/<u>blood splattered</u> to have been responsible for the <u>repeated multiple injuries</u>,

particularly when

(5) the Police apparently took 10 days before deciding it was <u>the</u> murder weapon

and

(6) no asbestos fibres or horse hairs have been found in the 13 wounds submitted to the W.M.F.S.L.

Bibliography

Archives

The National Archives, Kew
West Yorkshire Police Archives

Books

Burn, Gordon, *Somebody's Husband, Somebody's Son: The Story of the Yorkshire Ripper* (paperback, Faber and Faber, London, 4 March 2004)
Clark, Chris and Tate, Tim, *Yorkshire Ripper – The Secret Murders: The True Story of Serial Killer Peter Sutcliffe's Reign of Terror* (John Blake Publishing, London, 29 June 2015)
Jones, Barbara, *Voices from an Evil God: The True Story of the Yorkshire Ripper and the Woman Who Loved Him* (Blake Publishing, London, 1991)
Lee, Carol Ann, *Somebody's Mother, Somebody's Daughter: True Stories from Victims and Survivors of the Yorkshire Ripper* (Michael O'Mara Books, London, 2019)
Thurber, James, *The Secret Life of Walter Mitty* (*The New Yorker*, New York United States, March 1939)

Magazines and Newspapers

Aberdeen Evening Press
   (19 May 1979)
Birmingham Daily Post
Birmingham Evening Mail
   (Articles dated Saturday, 10 June 1972 and Monday, 11 June 1972)

Daily Express
   (5 April 1973)
Daily Mirror
   (https://www.mirror.co.uk/news/uk-news/yorkshire-ripper-survivor-had-home-14142649)
Daily Star
   (Friday, 9 June 2000)
Keighley News
Police Gazette
Real Crime, Future Plc
Sunday Mercury
Tamworth Herald
   (Friday, 23 June 1972 and Friday, 30 June 1972)
The Guardian
   (Interview between Andrew James Evans and journalist Patick Weir, 2000)
The Independent
The Sentinel

Online Sources

Daily Mirror
   (https://www.mirror.co.uk/news/uk-news/yorkshire-ripper-survivor-had-home-14142649)
Wikipedia

Television Programmes

Associated Television reconstruction footage of Barbara Mayo's journey, Associated Television
Crime Stalker, (Carlton Television), Central Television, 1994
Crimewatch, BBC, 1991
Crimewatch Roadshow, BBC, 2018
ITN news footage, ITN, 1972
The Nightmare, 1997

The One Show, BBC
Yorkshire Ripper: The Secret Murders, Impossible Factual and ITV
Silent Victims: The Untold Story of The Yorkshire Ripper (documentary), Network First, 1996
Sky News, Sky

Interviews Undertaken by the Authors

Interview with Dr Stuart Hamilton, Home Office registered forensic pathologist.
Interview with 'Officer A', 2020.

Police Interviews and Statements

Extracts of statements made by DI Keith Houlston and DC Charles Bowyer.
Extracts from statement made by DCI Stanley Wood at police headquarters, Stafford.
Interview by DCS Harold Wright (head of CID, Staffordshire Police) and DCS Saunders (of New Scotland Yard) with Andrew Evans, Tamworth Police Station, Wednesday, 11 October 1972, 8.50 am.
Extracts from statement by DCS Harold Wright (head of CID, Staffordshire Police).
Extracts from interview by DC Kenneth Peach (of Longton Police Station, Stoke-on-Trent) and DS Roy Williamson (of Hanley Police Station, Staffordshire) with Andrew Evans, Sunday, 8 October 1972, 9.00 pm.

Court Appearances

Birmingham Crown Court, Birmingham, June 1973
    (Andrew Evans' trial)
    (Tuesday, 3 April 1973 Andrew Evans' trial commences)
    (9 and 10 April 1973 Andrew Evans gives evidence at his trial)
Old Bailey Crown Court, 1981
    (Peter Sutcliffe's trial)
Court of Appeal

(Andrew Evans' appeal)

Prisons and Psychiatric Hospitals

Broadmoor, Berkshire: Peter Sutcliffe was a patient and housed in the Dangerous Severe Personality Disorder unit between 1984 and 2016.

HMP Frankland, Durham: Peter Sutcliffe served time in this prison following his stay at Broadmoor.

HMP The Verne, Dorset: Andrew Evans served time in this prison.

Reports

The Byford Report, 1981; carried out by the Home Office.

The Keith Hellawell Investigation, 1981–1992; ordered by Colin Sampson and continued by Hellawell while he was chief constable of West Yorkshire Police.

The Sampson Report, 1981; undertaken by West Yorkshire Police.

Images and Photographs

All images and photographs included in the plate section include an appropriate credit to the copyright holders.

Index

Aberdeen Evening Press, 81
Ansell-Lamb, Jacqueline 'Jacqui' Susan, 153, 155, 160, 165, 202
Atkinson, Patricia 'Tina', 52, 68–70, 77

Bakewell, 152, 202–203
Bexley Psychiatric Hospital, 152, 166–7
Birdsall, Trevor, 160, 54–5
Bingham, Lord Chief Justice Lord, 168–9, 195
Bingley, 1, 50, 55, 63, 72, 158, 162–3, 204
Birmingham, 2–4, 6, 149
Birmingham Crown Court, xx, 136, 143, 169
Birmingham Daily Post, 198
Birmingham Evening Mail, 15–16, 141
Boreham, Mr Justice, 81, 163, 166
Bonn, Dr Scott, 157
Bowyer, DC, 93–7, 100–102
Bradford, xvii, 50, 53, 66, 68, 70, 72, 74, 78, 81, 166–7, 199–200, 202
Bradford Police Station, 57
Brown, Mr Justice Douglas, 169
Browne, Tracy, 62, 65, 203
Bunce, Mr Bernard, 136

Burke, Marie, 153, 165–6
Byford Report, The, xiii, xiv, 59, 62, 209

Chichton, Mr Justice, 136
Claxton, Marcella, 67–9
Colclough, DC, 102–103, 105–107, 121–2
Cooper, Paul, 91–3
Court of Appeal, xxi, 168, 201

Dailly, Ann, 45–7
Daily Express, 23, 139
Daily Star, 197
Darby, Christine Ann, 6–9
Deptford, 80, 158
Derbyshire, xvii, 1, 20, 28, 152–3, 155, 159, 161, 162, 198, 202
Dinsdale, DS Ernest, 92–3
Downing, Stephen, xvii, 196, 203–204

Evans, Andrew James, xvii–xxi, 36, 83–5, 87–9, 92–7, 100–108, 110, 112–51, 168–9, 175, 185, 195–7, 210–11, 214
Evans, Bertha, 14
Evans, Irene, 83, 141
Evans, Joan, 138

Frankland, HMP, xiii

Gibbens, Mr Brian, 136, 139–40, 144–7, 150
Gibson, Private Barrie Keith, 16–18, 143
Gloucestershire Regiment, 83

Halifax, 61, 77, 160
Hamilton, Dr Stuart, 28–30, 32–7
Hill, Jaqueline, 58, 80
Hoban, DCS Dennis, 66
Home Office, xiii–iv, xxi, 20, 25, 28, 39, 59, 98, 138–9, 196, 200, 205
Houlston, DI, 93–7, 100–102
Huddersfield, 74, 80

Jackson, Emily, 52, 65–8, 70, 77
Jordan, DSI Frank, 20, 52, 69
Jordan, Jean, 70–2, 199, 202
Jowitt, Mr Justice, 169

Lea, Maureen 'Mo', 79
Leach, Barbara, 52, 59, 64, 78–80
Leeds, 64, 66–9, 79–80, 203
Lichfield, xix, 4–5, 16, 20, 25, 49, 96, 105, 107, 130, 170, 177
London, 4, 20, 67, 70–1, 81, 152–4, 157–60, 162–7
Long, Maureen, 68–9
Longton Police Station, xx, 84, 87, 91, 102, 108, 110, 119–20, 170, 172

Manchester, 7, 59, 69, 72, 153–4
Mayo, Barbara, 153, 159–62, 165, 202
McCann, Wilma, 52, 64–6, 68–9, 73, 80, 139

McDonald, Jayne, 52, 68, 70
Millward, Vera, 52, 76, 165
Moore, Marilyn, 69, 73
Morris, Raymond Leslie, 8–9, 12

New Scotland Yard, 7–9, 25, 39, 57–8, 65, 127, 134, 141, 143, 199, 206

O'Connor, DCS Terrance, 169, 188, 192, 194–5, 199
Ogden, Private Peter Raymond, 140
Owen, Mr John, 136–8, 140, 143–4, 147–9, 185

Peach, DC Kenneth, 87–9, 113–19
Pearson, Yvonne, 52, 73–4, 79, 200, 206
Prince, DC Ephraim, 20–1, 25

Rees, Chief Constable Arthur, 19–20
Richardson, Irene, 52, 68–70, 165
Roberts, Ann, 12–13, 16, 24, 143
Roberts, Judith, x–xxi, 12–38, 45–51, 56, 82–7, 98, 110, 113, 135–9, 141–7, 149, 168–9, 171, 184, 190–1, 196–200, 202, 206, 209–14
Roberts, Judy, 12–14, 16
Roberts, Vincent, 12, 14–15, 22
Robinson's Field, 17, 20, 23, 25, 31–2, 38, 45, 76, 143, 169–70, 175, 178–9, 185
Rogulskyj, Anna, 58–9, 65, 204, 209
Rytka, Helen, 73–5

Saunders, DCS Donald, 24–5, 40, 49, 84, 127–8, 141–4
Scotland Yard, 24
Sewell, Wendy, 152, 196, 202, 205–206

Smelt, Olive, 61–5, 67, 80, 204
St Albans, 153, 165–6
St Ives, 153
Staffordshire, 1–7, 9–12, 16, 25, 169, 198
   Police, 15, 18–20, 36, 51, 58, 83, 87–8, 127, 196, 206, 210, 212–13
Steel, Anthony, xvii, 200–201
Steele, Lance Corporal Trevor George, 16–18
Stephens, Dr Anton, 148, 184
Stewart, DCI, 118, 134
Sunday Mercury, 24
Sutcliffe, Peter, ix–xviii, 50–82, 139, 152, 155, 158, 160–67, 199–209, 213–14
Sutcliffe, Sonia, *see* Szurma, Sonia
Sykes, Theresa, 78
Szurma, Sonia, 53–4, 81–2, 152, 158, 162–7, 200

Tamworth, xix, 2–5, 12–13, 20–1, 23, 25, 38, 85, 87, 91–6, 101–104, 107–108, 111, 119–20, 127–30, 134, 142–4, 169, 172–3, 175, 177, 197–8

Police Station, 39, 132, 134
Tamworth Herald, 47–8

van der Merwe, Dr, 20–1, 23, 25–31, 33–5, 78, 138–9

Walls, Marguerite, 52, 59, 79
Washbrook, Dr Reginald, 149–50, 180, 183–4, 187
West Yorkshire, 59, 61–2, 64, 66–70, 76, 80, 163
West Yorkshire Police, xiii–xvi, 64, 66, 201, 206
Whitaker, Josephine, 52, 77–9, 160–1, 165
Whittington Barracks, xix, 15–16, 83–4, 95, 104–105, 107, 128, 131, 133, 170
Wilkinson, Carol, 11, 195, 200–201, 206
Williamson, DS Roy, 87–9, 111–13, 118–19
Wood, DCI Stanley, 102–108, 111, 119, 121–9, 132, 134, 141
Wright, DCS, 19–20, 23, 25–6, 39, 48–9, 84, 127–8, 141